THE INVISIBLE CROWN

THE INVISIBLE CROWN

A story of Dorothy von Flüe

- Wife of the patron saint of Switzerland -

Adapted to English
by

MICHAEL McGRADE

THE SAINT AUSTIN PRESS
296 Brockley Road
London SE4 2RA
Tel +44 (0) 181 692 6009
Fax +44 (0) 181 469 3609

Email: books@saintaustin.org
http://www.saintaustin.org

THE INVISIBLE CROWN

A story of Dorothy von Flüe
- Wife of the patron saint of Switzerland -

Adapted to English by **MICHAEL McGRADE**

From the original German:
"Verborgene Krone" by **MICHAEL JUNGO OSB**
[Titel der deutschen Originalausgabe: Jungo, Verborgene Krone,
Christiana-Verlag, CH-8260 Stein am Rhein/Schweiz]
and the French: *"La Couronne Invisible"*
[Eric E. Thilo, Editions St-Paul, Freiburg, 1958]

Cover: *The Parting* by Kazia Olszta (© 1999)
Photos: Josef Reinhard, Sachseln (pp.42, 43, 71, 72, 73, 95)
Carl Abächerli, Sarnen (p.44)
Leonhard von Matt, Buochs (p.96)

A catalogue record for this book is available from the British Library.

ISBN 1 901157 76 8

CONTENTS

ACKNOWLEDGEMENTS

To Irene Bissig, who led me to Nicholas and Dorothy; to my brother-in-law, Peter Collecott, whose unflagging kindness and hospitality made this work possible; to David and Mary Selby, whose godly generosity brought it to fruition – my eternal gratitude.

This book
is dedicated to the
greatest of all Divine gifts
- the Most Blessed Sacrament of the Altar -
and to the mother of all virtues
- obedience -
in the hope that those who have
grown indifferent to the former
and forgotten the latter
may regain their love
for both.

PREFACE

St. Nicholas von Flüe, the patron saint of Switzerland, is barely known outside that diminutive country. His wife, Dorothy, even less so. Given the incomparable array of Catholic saints, each of whose life of service to others and particular gifts seem more remarkable than the other, perhaps this is not surprising. We cannot be familiar with each of them - more's the pity! But for all that, it is most unfortunate that this extraordinary couple are not better known in the English-speaking world, since the crucial virtues they so courageously embraced and taught are now universally lacking, to the detriment of society at every level. And nowhere is this deficiency and its dislocating effect more evident than within the Holy Catholic Church itself, as was the case during the von Flüe's lifetime in 15th century Europe, on the eve of the first Reformation.

Five hundred years on, my first book, *Death of a Catholic Parish: The Benalla Experiment (DCP)*, dealt with the next instalment: REFORMATION II - providing a first-hand look at the state of Catholic life common throughout Western countries in the death-throes of the 20th century. It is not a pretty sight! Priestly dissent, episcopal complicity, scandal, disunity, acrimony... the depressingly familiar list goes on. In examining this ugly reality, *DCP* attempted to instruct and encourage faithful Catholic's faced with a second-wave of Protestantisation. During the controversy that raged in the wake of the book's publication, however, it became clear that a somewhat different approach was now needed to reinforce the heart of the message it contained. For the ongoing Benalla tragedy, as with the Catholic crisis in general, is in essence a matter of missing virtues - two in particular. And what more edifying example could be given to demonstrate the need for those missing virtues, and the rewards when practised, than that embodiment of virtue and living example par excellence - a Catholic saint.

Never outdone in generosity, Divine Providence ultimately led me to *two* saints - one formally canonised, the other just as surely ensconced in that elect company. In the lives of St. Nicholas von Flüe and his spouse Dorothy, I discovered a worthy sequel to *DCP* – a sure antidote to the disease that has infected and emaciated parishes, seminaries and religious houses for three decades. For if it is true that the "missing virtues" at the very heart of Reformation II are *obedience* and *reverence*, then Klaus and Dorothy provide a timely reminder of the absolute necessity of these virtues in re-establishing lasting peace and unity within each parish community and thus throughout the universal Church and the world.

In Father Michael Jungo's deceptively simple, uplifting interpretation of the life of Dorothy von Flüe, *Verbogene Krone,* I found a captivating vehicle for conveying the desired message. Yet, as admirably as the book achieved this purpose in a way accessible to young and old alike, it left one wanting further detail and counsel from St. Nicholas himself - about whom, it soon became evident, there was an astonishing lack of available information. And so I headed for Europe, where a wealth of Brother Klaus literature in German and French, plus one lone and invaluable English source, has enabled me to sketch a historical portrait of St. Nicholas - included in the Appendices - to both complement and enhance *The Invisible Crown.*

Taken as a whole, this work, set in a distant yet disturbingly familiar age, provides the reader with an inexhaustible well of ideas upon which to reflect and pray - such as Klaus' statement that *"obedience is the greatest glory that there is in heaven and on earth... ."* He and his wife lived by that dictum and an entire country was rewarded and unified through it; just as surely as clerical disobedience - whether in improvisations at the altar during Holy Mass or failure to preach and teach precisely with the Church or in worldly attire and behaviour - has been rewarded with division, disunity and scandal today. And the greatest scandal is not the consequent encroachment of vice and perversion, which has led many clerics to grace lascivious newspaper headlines around the world. More distressing by far is the further damage such disobedience has wrought on the crucial virtue of reverence in an already irreverent world. Within the Catholic realm, the Blessed Sacrament has suffered even more heinously than the priesthood itself.

This particular irreverence, now endemic among the faithful, is manifested in the total disregard of the Real Presence of Our Lord and God in the tabernacles of our churches. Instead of awe and silence before this greatest of mysteries, we find: constant chattering, even and especially among the middle-aged and elderly, as if the church was merely an extension of the parish hall; a repulsive familiarity with the sacred displayed by so many priests, altar servers and laity in their slovenly comportment on the sanctuary; a general lack of decorum by all and sundry before the tabernacle; and an unthinkable nonchalance in the handling of the Blessed Eucharist which contains the Body, Blood, Soul and Divinity of Our Lord and Saviour Jesus Christ.

Those among us honest enough to admit that they have fallen prey to such abominable behaviour might reflect on the particular miracle visited on St. Nicholas by God and thus regain the necessary internal and external dispositions required in a Catholic church where Our Lord resides **physically** in the consecrated Host. For those prepared to meditate on the miracle and the words of the saint and truly enter into themselves on this point, it may even convince them to re-think their decision to receive Communion in the hand – presently legitimate but surely a less humble and reverential gesture towards the Lord than receiving on the tongue. The clergy too may once again be persuaded that the central position formerly accorded the Blessed Sacrament on our sanctuaries is more appropriate for Our Lord and King than a mere side-chapel.

As readers ponder these and many other points which present

themselves for consideration in the following pages, they will also be reassured to find that Dorothy and Nicholas well understood the doubts and difficulties experienced by souls trying to live their Faith in a deeply troubled Church. Nicholas states at one point: *"Many people are in a state of doubt about their Faith and the devil makes many attacks on faith - above all in this matter of faith. We must not be in any doubt, for the Faith is as it has been revealed."*

Clearly this blessed couple have much to teach us about that Holy Faith to which St. Nicholas refers, once again under attack from lax and worldly bishops, priests and religious, busily mimicking their pre-Reformation forebears to such devastating effect on the life of the Church and souls. Yet they also speak to those outside the Catholic fold and it would be a tragedy if their message was discarded simply because essential parts of their history seem too incredible to the modern, secular mind - more attuned as it is to UFO's, Reincarnation and Fate than Catholic miracles, the Resurrection and Divine Providence.

"If people don't believe in God," it is said, "they won't believe in nothing; they'll believe in anything!" Anything *except*, it seems, the claims of the Catholic Church! In view of this prevailing attitude, it is important to establish from the outset the other-worldly aspect of Catholic life that courses through the almost surreal human drama which follows, so that interested non-Catholics might approach and study it from the right perspective. To this end, a brief history of Anna Melchior of Klangenfurt, Austria, is helpful.

By the age of 45, Anna had been bed-ridden for twelve years with tuberculosis of the spine, paralysis, subsidiary infections and painful complications. A Swiss woman resident in Klangenfurt gave her a picture of Blessed Klaus von Flüe together with a book about him containing some of his prayers and a short account of his life. This introduction to Brother Klaus made a deep impression on her. She did not pray for specific favours but found comfort and strength in an inward communion with him.

In May 1947 she was so ill that the end seemed imminent; she was quite ready to die, thankful that this would relieve the strain on her ageing mother who had been nursing her at home for the past 10 years. At this time, she chanced to see the following headline in a Catholic paper which her mother had put down on her bed: *"The Pope has elevated the Swiss farmer Nicholas von Flüe to the honour of sainthood."* After reading this, Anna, with great effort, raised her one good arm to stroke the picture of Brother Klaus which hung near her bed, and said: "Saint Brother Klaus, I congratulate you." She later described the experience which followed as an extraordinary sensation, like an electric current coursing through every limb. She literally threw off the bedclothes, jumped out of bed and started to walk out of the room in her nightgown. At that moment, her mother arrived with two female visitors who had come to pay their last respects to the dying invalid. The first words Anna recalls from the three flabbergasted women were: "You'll catch cold!" The date was 15 May, 1947 - the day of the canonisation ceremony in Rome.

Anna Melchior was completely cured and lived a normal, active life for many years thereafter. Her moving story and post-war journey of thanksgiving to St. Nicholas' hermitage in central Switzerland, is related in Ida Lüthold-Minder's *Vom Himmel beglaubigt.*

Although not articles of Faith which must be believed, such regularly occurring, verifiable miracles throughout a two-thousand year period - often more astonishing than physical cures and all simply beyond the realms of science - are nothing if not persuasive pointers to the divine nature of the Catholic Church. To the non-believer, therefore, the point is made that Anna Melchior's instantaneous and total recovery is a part of that supernatural, sacramental life of grace and invisible realities in which Catholic's dwell and go about their daily business. It is a world where events of the most extraordinary kind can and do happen, as and when it pleases the one, true God Who surely guides all human life and history, just as He leaves each and every person free to accept or reject Himself and His Church of Rome - the conduit for His grace and teachings on earth *[Matt. 16:18-20]*. It is the world in which the subjects of this work lived and breathed and acted out their eternal destiny. They carry a divine message for each member of our tormented age - Dorothy no less than St. Nicholas himself.

Described by John Paul II as a man who *"took the words of the Gospel literally!... a genuine witness of Christ! A person who fulfilled the Gospel to the last word,"* Brother Klaus may at first glance appear to overwhelm and dwarf the figure of his wife. An illusion firmly rejected by two pontiffs.

At the time of his canonisation, addressing Swiss pilgrims, Pope Pius XII thanked Dorothy for her contribution to her husband's spiritual and temporal mission: *"Today, in this solemn hour, his wife's name also deserves honourable mention. She contributed through the voluntary renunciation of her husband - a renunciation that was not easy for her - and through her sensitive, genuinely Christian attitude in the years of separation, to give you the saviour of the Fatherland and the saint."*

During his visit to Switzerland in June 1984, Pope John Paul II confirmed these sentiments at the grave of Brother Klaus in the Sachseln parish church, where he prayed:

"My Lord and my God,... thanks to your gracious Providence Brother Klaus found in Dorothy an understanding spouse, who prayed and struggled with him for the strength to obey Your Divine Will. You called Dorothy in place of her husband to assume responsibility for family, house and farm, so that the way of the saint became free for life in The Ranft, free for prayer, free for Your mission to establish peace... With Brother Klaus and his devout wife Dorothy let us more and more realise that genuine reconciliation and lasting peace comes from You alone."

If Dorothy's *"fiat mihi"* echoed Mary's salvific response, a sword likewise pierced her heart. And while the Blessed Mother is bound intimately and forever to the redemptive work of her Son, so too Dorothy's sacrifice is inseparable from the saving, peacemaking role of her spouse. As Father Josef Oberwiler, the Brother Klaus Chaplain in Sachseln, wrote to me: "without her courageous response, there would be no Brother Klaus, no Ranft, no Covenant of Stans." In the deepest sense Dorothy moved above and beyond her natural role as mother of ten children to become the spiritual mother of a nation. For the loftiest apostolate of woman in the Church and the world exceeds biological motherhood; it is the religious mission entrusted to her by the Creator and embodied in the maternity of the Blessed Virgin - to lead souls to God. As her *"fiat"* resounds across the centuries, Dorothy pursues that divine charge still - in eternity. I hope and pray that this modest work, in some small measure, will aid her cause.

West Sussex, 1998.

"A VIRTUOUS WOMAN IS HER HUSBAND'S CROWN"

Proverbs 12:4

PART I

CROWN OF FLOWERS

It was the year 1446, the first Tuesday of Lent.

The day broke to the sounding of the tocsin - the alarm-bell! From Sarnen, up and down the valley the frightening echo advanced, relentlessly, from steeple to steeple and even to the mountains, where the shrill voice of solitary chapel bells responded to its baleful message. In the homes, women fell to their knees before the crucifix; men furbished axes and pikes. Abandoned children howled.

At the "Neuhof," high up on Mount Schwändi on the sunny side of the Sarnen valley, where the highly respected Wyss family had dwelt since time immemorial, news of the war had arrived several hours before. The master of the house, Councillor Ruedi Wyss, had brought it himself. In an instant, the comfortable household day-dreaming under its heavy blanket of snow had succumbed to agitation.

In the loft, Father Wyss and his two oldest sons were inspecting their weapons; the mother was at the hearth roasting oats for the men and had directed the maid to fetch down the fattest ham from the chimney. But it was the children who most gave of themselves: the boys occupied in oiling their brother's helmets; the girls in mending and brushing their doublets and satchels. The whole household was one of comings and goings, shouts and hubbub!

The eldest daughter, an elegant girl with rounded features and thick, blond plaits - she would be fifteen at Easter - went quietly about her work, trying to hide her reddened eyes. She had been crying; yet no one, at the time, had been aware of it. Her mother alone had sensed her distress and called her into the kitchen.

"Come," she said, stroking her velvet hair, "help me to prepare the dough."

While they were working alone together, there came an impetuous knock at the door.

"Klaus!" gasped the girl softly, blushing all over.

"Dorothy!" he returned, and his sharp, tanned features darkened a little more.

She remained as if paralysed behind the kitchen table; he, motionless in the open doorway. It was the mother who exorcised them, going to meet him and offering her flour-whitened hands.

"This accursed, fratricidal war," she sighed by way of hello, "when will it ever finish?"

"I only came to say goodbye," said Sergeant von Flüe evasively. "Since one never knows...," he added with an embarrassed air. His eyes met those of the young girl, which suddenly overflowed with tears. He took a step towards her, but stopped half-way and starred blankly at the glowing embers in the fireplace.

"We've completely forgotten Father's doublet!" exclaimed the mother and went out.

Klaus and Dorothy remained alone. She stood, eyes lowered, kneading the dough with all her might and bathing it in her tears. He stepped closer, lifted his hand to calm her but dared not touch the silken hair.

"If God wills, I'll return!" he said in a hushed voice.

When she continued crying, he said: "You'll be my angel in

battle - think of me, Dorothy!"

At last she looked up at him and the tearful eyes brightened momentarily before, all at once, the door flew open and the two eldest boys stormed through in a fracas of heavy clogs.

"Not yet on the way, Sergeant, Sir?" teased one. The other slapped Klaus heartily on the shoulder and said excitedly: "We'll give these cursed Zurich men a taste of blood and dust!"

Von Flüe did not respond but simply asked: "Are you ready?"

"As soon as Father is!"

At that moment the Father walked through the door. His worried look brightened at the sight of the young man and, smiling, he extended his hand. He then turned to his daughter, still standing behind the table, brushed aside a tuft of hair from her forehead and said: "Don't cry child! If you pray, you and your mother, we'll return from this safe and sound."

After the boys brought in the helmets and spears and the girls had hung the satchels about them, they went out into the snow and the glistening afternoon light.

While Father Wyss took leave of his family, Klaus and Dorothy stood aside. As the girl looked down at the snow, the faraway eyes of the young man caressed the slender, childlike silhouette of his betrothed. Eventually, he composed himself and took her hand without a word.

"God be with you!" she sobbed.

He turned away resolutely and signalled to the waiting group to set off...

Long after the four men had disappeared into the black pine forest, the two women, Mother Anna and young Dorothy, were still standing by the hedge near the small, babbling spring water fount, looking into the valley. The first warm February sun was setting behind them. Above, in the light blue, the snow-covered mountaintops shimmered a delicate crimson. A light mist veiled the lake and valley floor.

It was all so grave and still that it seemed impossible that, over there, behind the jagged contours of Mount Pilatus, horror and death threatened.

The St Niklausen Angelus bells began to ring, thin and silvery. Dorothy lifted her head and looked across to the old spire relaying the divine message. Then her eyes slid lower, to where an unfinished shingle roof gleamed between the trees: the home that Klaus was building specially for her! She threw herself into her mother's arms: "Oh Mother, Mother!" she groaned.

"They'll be home again!" came the soothing reply. "Father has already been called away many times. Long ago, in the Spring, when your Grandfather died - you were still in the cradle! Again, in that year when the harvest was so poor, and then a few days after the barn burnt down! We were scarcely married when he had to cross the Saint-Gothard pass, where our men were beaten terribly by the Duke of Milan's mercenaries; but your Father returned from it and without a single wound."

The mother became pensive and looked down towards Alpnach, where mountainous folds released a view of Lake Lucerne.

"Do you remember when he returned from Basel, two years ago, from the battle of St Jakob on the Birse, with that deep shoulder wound? He came through that alive too!"

She fell silent. After a while, she whispered again, more for herself than for her daughter: "Times are hard. Death reaps the men and leaves the women alone, to wait.... Well, either way, God wants to find us ready!" she added softly and, so saying, put her hand on her daughter's shoulder and guided her gently into the house.

During the night, as everyone slept, Dorothy slipped out of bed and tiptoed to the window, opened it wide and looked out at the star filled sky. Beyond, against the luminous snow, glowed the sanctuary lamp of Our Lady of Schwändi. Eyes focused steadfastly on the little red star, she repeated again and again the same fervent prayer: "Dear, beloved, Mother of God, You protect my Nicholas for me!"

In her grief, this little "my" seemed especially sweet and it did her heavy heart good to confide her young love to Our Lady.

Then she went back to bed and slowly found peace in a deep, dreamless sleep.

*   *   *

They were married at the beginning of May. Summer had quickly passed and one already fresh September evening, Dorothy was seated in the kitchen of her new home - which still smelt of resin and fresh paint. Nicholas was in the cowshed busily milking the cows. Outside, the first autumn storm raged. The Melchaa torrent rushed and thundered and the three old fir trees behind the house groaned in the furious wind.

Dorothy had never felt as cosy in her home as now, listening to the storm break in vain against its walls. She felt perfectly secure under that familiar roof Klaus had built for her, before the hearth he had entrusted to her and which, at night, she covered with ashes so that it never entirely died.

As the tempest shook the windows, she stirred the gruel in her little cooking-pot. Now and again, she wiped away the tears forced from her smoke-filled eyes. Then she stopped, watched the licking flames and listened blissfully to a new life beating within her.

Her thoughts often wandered back to that day filled with the scent of hay, gladdened by brilliant flowers and the twittering of birds, when with trembling heart she had pledged herself forever. She thought of the old parish priest who had blessed her marriage. She saw again his features, wrinkled as an apple, and heard his voice, made gravelly and faltering by the weight of years.

In his earthy way, the reverent man of God had told her that marriage is like a hen house: those outside want to get in - God alone knows why! - those inside, want to get out! which in the end, the Devil might explain better than the Good Lord Himself!

Dorothy had well understood the desire of the hens wanting to enter the cage. But that, once inside, the dumb things cackled wildly, pecked each other and wanted to get out again - that was simply beyond her comprehension!

She was happy with her husband; what more could she want? Had he not awakened her from the slumber of her maidenhood and led her into a world more wonderful than her wildest dreams? He had revealed to her the beauty of nature, the unfathomable depths of the human heart, and when he spoke of God it was as if she was discovering Him for the first time! She was his attentive pupil and he had so formed her soul that she could only say to him, with a sense of overwhelming gratitude: "It is no longer me, but *you* living in me!"

It was clear that she would never want to leave her "cage" - but him? What did she have to hold him? And how could she thank him for all that he gave her daily? Yet today, she *did* know what to give him: this new heart already beating below her own, a living gift more precious than all the gifts that men had ever made! Especially today, on the Feast of St Gallus, to whom he was so devoted, she wanted to reveal her secret to him.

The door opened and Klaus entered quietly, hay still clinging to his hair. Trying to muffle the sound of his clogs, he advanced towards his wife. The closer he got, the more his stern features lit up into a broad smile. He stopped a moment, and in the glow of the flames contemplated with tenderness the smooth, almost childlike nape of her neck. Shyly, he laid his hands upon her shoulders and felt the gentle shiver of her frame under his warm touch.

It was she who broke the intimate silence: "Sit here next to me, Nicholas, I have something... for you."

"How very mysterious you are," he replied, amused. "One would almost think you've got a great secret in store for me."

As he took his place, full of expectation, he caught a strange glimmer in her eyes. Enthralled, he gazed at the wondrous union of her soft, full mouth and the pensive smile. And when her hands moved protectively to her heart, he understood. Yet it was for her to speak and with baited breath, he waited.

"You know, Nicholas," she finally said, "God has decided... that we shouldn't be alone... ." A hot flame rushed to her brow. She lowered her eyes, yet immediately searched for his. But he had already taken her hands, raising them to his lips. "Oh Dorothy!" he exclaimed, "We must thank God for His grace!" And the blue of his eyes became deeper still.

Dorothy expected the child by Candlemas. But at Candlemas it had not arrived. Another full, anxious week passed before the appearance of a vigorous baby boy. They named him John, after the disciple whom Jesus loved, and at home simply called him Hans.

Throughout those last days, she had waited with nervous impatience for the first pangs of childbirth and then, for hours, had swallowed her cries while her body heaved in pain. Finally, hair wet with perspiration, she lay bloodless on the fresh linen - until sheer happiness renewed her strength and, eyes aglow, she pointed her husband to the small, white bundle. Nicholas, however, saw only her and a sharp light in his eyes thanked her. He then turned cautiously towards the cradle and with his callused farmer's hands, made the first sign of the cross on this fruit of their love.

An air of tenderness and charm filled the home. The rugged father was moved at the sight of the wriggling miracle. He looked in awe at the delicacy and precision of the little ears and hands and the tiny nails. And so it was with the wife. When she looked at the child by her side, it was to her as a fleeting reflection of a divine and distant smile. The day his small, precious face grinned awkwardly for the first time, she knew bliss in its plenitude.

*   *   *

It was Christmas Eve. Klaus was in the stable feeding the animals. Dorothy had just started taking some crusty cakes and pastries from the hot stove when there was a fierce knocking at the door. Carefully, the young woman took the candlestick from the chimney and went to open. Outside stood her father's stable boy, pale from fatigue and blue with cold.

"I must...," he stuttered, before gushing: "Come quick something's happened to your Father in the forest at the lumbering."

She took a breath.

"Is he dead?"

Without waiting for a response she added hurriedly: "Come here near the fire, you're half frozen!"

Soon Klaus and Dorothy found themselves on the path to Schwändi. On the way, Nicholas wanted a detailed explanation of the accident but the poor fellow could repeat nothing other than: "He wanted to save me and fell under the tree himself...I would have been no great loss!"

During the trek, they saw from afar all the lights burning in the solitary farm. The dog howled dismally. At the house, some neighbours stood waiting in the narrow passageway but parted respectfully when they recognised the lofty figure of Councillor von Flüe.

Dorothy went up immediately to her father's room. Subdued murmurs and a bloody odour greeted her at the door. A muffled groan made her shudder. From the doorway, she saw her Father lying there, disfigured; for an instant she stood petrified, then threw herself on her knees next to the bed. A whisper passed among those present as each well knew she was the favourite daughter of the dying.

Pale, nose pinched, he lay in the heavy pillows. His hair was clammy and blood ran from his wound on the back of his head through the reddened bandage and seeped into the grey linen. He struggled for air and his eyes already groped in the darkness.

Dorothy had clutched his hand and was pressing it incessantly to her lips. At the same time, she fixed her gaze upon his features and caressed the back of his coarse hand with her soft fingertips. The warm contact seemed to calm him and his eyes searched for the one who brought him such relief.

Mother Wyss leaned over and whispered Dorothy's name in his ear. His mouth contorted in an onerous smile and with a deep sigh he turned his head a little, so that the wound bled with renewed vigour. Seeing that he wanted to speak, she brought her ear closer to his lips. "Be good to Klaus," he whispered, "he needs you!" After a fit of coughing, which nearly choked him, he gasped laboriously: "Stand firm together, you two!" Then he fell back exhausted.

The priest, who had since arrived, read in his features the signs of impending death. They lit two candles and in a monotone voice he commenced the Last Rites. The flames always threatened to expire in the thick air of the small bedroom, which smelt of damp clothes, sweat and blood. In a corner, someone wept.

Suddenly, the heavy body shuddered. Father Wyss opened his eyes wide; his expression froze. The clergyman drew a final, large sign of the cross over him; the oldest son closed the dead man's eyes.

It was already close to midnight when Klaus and Dorothy set out on the way home. Huddled together, they waded through the fresh, powdery snow.

"What did Father mean?" the woman repeatedly asked herself, turning over his mysterious last words in her head. Was it really true that Klaus needed her? Had they till now not been close enough?

While they were climbing to Flüe, silent with their heavy

burden, Klaus said unexpectedly, in a matter-of-fact way: "You know, tomorrow morning, at the first Holy Sacrifice, Father will be up above."

"How can you be so precise?" she said looking up at him, incredulous.

"God knows!" he replied.

Their ascent completed, he turned to her, took her by the shoulders and said slowly and thoughtfully: "Tonight I have become for you husband and brother and - father, my Dorli!"

He had scarcely pronounced the last word when the bells from St Niklausen began to sound for midnight Mass.

*   *   *

All the farmers of the Obwald, even those who only ever complained, agreed that the summer of 1459 was the most prolific they had known. Sun and rain vied with each other to ripen the harvest, the hay flourished and barns were scarcely able to hold the golden abundance. Housewives packed their cellars with juicy pears, blushing apples and vegetables galore. In the middle of the reaping, however, a heavy blow struck the von Flüe household.

On the night of the Feast of St Bartholomew, around morning, someone knocked violently on the door of the parental bedchamber. It was the eldest daughter, Verena, who called her mother urgently to little Elizabeth. Dorothy flew up the stairs into the girls' room and found the poor child in her cot, as pale as a corpse. She complained of stabbing pains around her abdomen. The mother felt the burning forehead, then the hands - they were completely frozen.

"Stay with her!" she said to her eldest. "And see that she's warm!" With that she raced to the kitchen and made a greenish broth.

When she again appeared under the low roof of the upstairs

room, where Verona had lit some candles, Dorothy was filled with dread. Her daughter's face had become transparent, bluish and stretched beyond recognition! She rushed to the cot and began to feel hand and foot, throat and shoulder of the sick. All limbs were as stiff as boards and pierced by convulsive spasms. For some seconds, the mother stood there bewildered and helpless; desperately she looked at her little Elizabeth, who stared wide-eyed at the ceiling. She shook the child, spoke to her and finally applied the steaming poultice to her stomach.

"Fetch Father!" she said to the impotent Verena kneeling beside her. In a daze, the girl went out.

"Lord God," implored the mother, "if it is Thy Holy Will... I will submit! But if it is possible, let this cup pass us by! Mother of Jesus and Our Mother, Mother of the Seven Sorrows, have pity on the poor child!... Yet, Lord, not my will, but Thine be done!"

As the gaunt figure of Klaus appeared in the doorway, a fierce jolt sped through the child's tormented frame. Her teeth clenched terribly and her little fingers dug into the sheet. All at once, the whole body arched, tightened and fell back in a heap.

Klaus rushed forward and mother and father held their child by the hands and shoulders. Dorothy wept and murmured incomprehensible pet names and words of affection. The father, overcome with grief, was speechless. One heard only the wheezing breath of the little girl and the indifferent gurgle of springwater in the garden.

The latch jangled and Hans, pail of milk in hand, looked in astonished. "Go quickly to old Martha!" the mother cried out to him, "and tell her that Betty is gravely ill and to come please with her roots!"

"That's pointless!" interrupted Nicholas. "Go instead to Kerns, to the priest, and ask him to come!"

Dorothy was silent. Hans disappeared.

It was broad daylight when the boy returned home bathed in perspiration. "The Reverend Father says that it's impossible for him to come now; also, that it's not necessary for a priest to be there for a dying child."

Klaus knew better. He bit his lips grimly, but said nothing.

"Lord, don't abandon us," pleaded Dorothy, laying the gold crucifix she wore on a little chain around her neck upon the bed of the dying.

The demise dragged on for three days and three nights. Dorothy fought the uneven battle between mother and death. What she would not have done to save this life she had brought into the world! And so she repeated endlessly: "My God, don't let her die. Take me in her place! But may Thy Will be done! Only give me the strength to accept it."

The powers of little Elizabeth diminished. With each passing hour the end drew closer.

On Saturday evening, the whole family was gathered around the bed save Walter, who was watering the horses. Dorothy's aged mother and her younger sister had come, both of whom were practised in nursing.

Elizabeth was calmer but her breathing threatened to stop at any moment. Some considerable time had passed when the aunt, standing at the head of the bed, said: "Pray! The end is near!" Everyone knelt down. Klaus lead the prayer: *"Pater Noster...,"* and at the end: *"In manum tuum Domine...* Into Thy hands, Lord, we commend her spirit."

An imperceptible tremble passed through the small, wasted body; the contorted features dissolved into a smile...the heart had stopped. The mother rose - tearless - and said: "I sewed your baptismal gown; I'll prepare your shroud." And she immediately set to work.

Three days later, when they returned from the graveyard, Dorothy fell exhausted into her husband's arms. For a long time they remained locked in embrace. Despite all the pain, Dorothy felt happy that in the trial Klaus had drawn closer to her, that they had become more intimately, truly, one.

*   *   *

The year 1460 was a troubled one. Tension, ferment and seething discontent reigned everywhere. Countless times Klaus was called away from the milking and ploughing to the Council or Tribunal. Often he did not return home till late, worn out and despondent. "Evil is just like a weed," he would often say, "you cut it, then it shoots up again a hundredfold!"

One evening, at the beginning of September, just as the sun descended behind the mountains, he came home breathless. Dorothy, recognising his step, went to him smiling. He did not look at her but said as he passed by: "May God help us! War has broken out again!" And he hurried to the armoury where his weapons were stored.

Dorothy sat down near the hearth and hid her face in her hands. But Walter, who was guarding the cows outside, ran in and cried excitedly: "Below in Sarnen there's a great red and white flag flying over the Town Hall!"

"Yes, child!" his mother replied, removing some straw from his wild locks, "it's the flag calling your Father to war... He's already there sharpening his sword." She pointed through an open window to the fount where the father was whetting the bluish steel.

The next morning, Klaus prepared for his departure in the main room. Hans, who already came up to his shoulders, helped him into his armour. Walter brought him sword and dagger. From his wife's hands he took his leather pouch and the new beret bearing red and white plumes - sign of his rank of Captain.

He caressed the two month old Anna, his youngest, who was brought in by the maid.

"Don't cry, Verena! I'm coming back again!" he said.

Then he traced a small cross on the forehead of his six children, extended both hands to his pale-faced wife and whispered in her ear: "God be with you, Dorothy."

Finally, he seized the long pike leaning against the doorpost and strode down into the valley, without once looking back.

Dorothy watched after him a long time, then took her youngest into the bedchamber, laid the child carefully in the cradle and sank to her knees before the cross. Soon, however, she remembered the children, dried her tears and went downstairs. She gathered everyone in the corner of the room in front of the large crucifix and began to pray with them: "Dear God. Thy Will be done in all things; but, if it is possible, save our good Father!"

The days passed. Cows descended from the high mountain pasture. Trees turned red and yellow; they lost their foliage and finally stood bare and desolate. The first autumn storms broke the deadwood from the treetops...

There was no news and Dorothy remained alone with her longings, alone with the same tormenting question: "Is he coming back? Will he come? Won't he come?"

At the end of October on the day before the first snow, Peter, Klaus' brother who was not called away because of his stiff leg, brought news that the Obwald banner had passed Frauenfeld and pushed as far as the Rhine. An indescribable joy reigned in the valley along with a feeling of confidence that the men would be home for winter.

In spite of that, Dorothy's heart was not quite able to rejoice. For her, the Rhine was the end of the world. She counted the days and weeks and it seemed to her that with each day the solitude and agony of the wait became more bitter still. Whenever her work permitted, she took her scarf and ran like a little girl to the Flüe pasture where the view plunged into the valley. There she looked out for a flag, listened for a drum roll - in vain!

Late one night, during the week after All Souls' Day, while scrubbing the cauldron, she heard some heavy, familiar steps outside the house. She leapt up quickly, arranged her clothes in ecstatic haste, and ran to the door. It was him.

"Klaus!" she stammered in her impetuous joy and buried herself in his embrace.

Since the household was already asleep, she bid him enter silently, took off his helmet and satchel and helped him to remove his armour. She then rekindled the fire and set about preparing supper.

As she ran busily from hearth to table, from table to hearth, she was troubled by his dogged silence.

"What's the matter?" she finally asked, setting down a steaming cabbage soup before him.

"Nothing... really!" he said dismissively. Yet she felt something was weighing on his soul and knew, too, that she alone could free him. And so she pressed him - now teasing, now serious - leaving him no peace.

"God forgive me!" he suddenly blurted, "for I fear that we are murderers!"

At these words she stopped dead, sat down opposite him and waited, eyes half-closed, for the next blow.

"I still see it before me, and every night I hear one of them whimper...

"It was beyond the Rhine, outside a small castle. We had stormed it and slaughtered nearly the whole garrison. The ten survivors, who still held the tower, had to surrender in their bare undershirts... In front of the whole assembled army, the executioner did his work...

"I still see one of them, the youngest; he barely had the first fluff on his chin. He screamed for his mother and struggled with all his might... At first they had to take him by the hair and shake him madly... "

As he spoke, Klaus had pulled some gold florins from his pocket. Now he hurled them onto the table and said with barely suppressed rage: "Is it not blood money?"

The woman stroked the soldier's unkempt hair. "Give that to the poor," he added, "I don't want it!"

He rose, looked towards the crucifix in the corner and implored: "Lord, turn away this bloody guilt from us and our children."

Dawn was already breaking when they lay down for a short sleep.

In late autumn of the following year, as the first crocus reared their sad little heads from the grass, Dorothy was seated one evening by the window, looking now and then towards the trail which emerged from the Melchtal forest. She was heavy with new life and busy sewing tiny dresses for her next child.

Outside, under the window, the two youngest were playing - Anna and Heini. With his dark eyes and unruly hair, Heini resembled Klaus. Pensively, the mother sat back and watched the boisterous youngster, one moment leaping after falling leaves, the next ripping out grass to feed his wooden cow, then guiding water from the fount into a little ditch he had dug in the ground.

"Just his father!" she thought proudly - and with that, an uncertain fear gripped her. Since returning from the last campaign, Klaus seemed to her to have changed. His mind was elsewhere... Had not the hay been brought in damp and was it not nearly rotten? Were not the pears still hanging here and there on the trees or falling overripe into the wet grass? And when she spoke to him about the regular work - about the honey that needed straining, the old boar that needed killing, or the apples to be urgently cut and dried - he took notice, but some graver concerns soon drove these small domestic worries from his mind.

One could not have said that he neglected his paternal duties but they had clearly become a burden for him. And it would also happen that, after several sleepless nights, one or other of the thousand minor details of daily farm work would escape his notice.

As Dorothy was pondering all this, she heard some urgent steps in the kitchen. The door flew open. Distressed and gasping for breath, Hans stood before her.

"In Heaven's name, Mother, come! Something has happened to Father!"

She dropped her work, rose cautiously and hurried to the kitchen. Peter and the farm-worker carried her husband over the stairs and into the hallway. Dorothy went ahead of them into the chamber, where they laid the injured man on the bed.

"What have you done Klaus?" she asked in bewilderment, looking at his bleached and bloodied face.

"Nothing, Dorothy, nothing... Look after yourself and the child!" he retorted and let his painfully uplifted head fall back on the pillow.

Dorothy quickly composed herself: she sent the two men out and had Verena bring some warm water and medicinal herbs, then undid the shirt and started cleansing his wounds. The upper part of the body seemed intact, but the right cheek was torn open and blood flowed down into his beard. The right foot was swollen and thoroughly blue. "What happened?" she asked anxiously after making sure that there was nothing broken.

"Oh, a fall, nothing more!" he answered.

Hans, however, who had returned in the meantime and was standing at the foot of the bed, declared: "The Evil One wanted to kill him, Mother!"

"It's not that bad," the father returned tranquilly. "Without God's permission he can't even harm one hair on our head, let alone kill us."

While Dorothy tended the sprained foot, Hans recounted the events.

They had arrived in the mist at their pasture above Melchtal just as the sun appeared behind Mount Geissberg. He had lit a fire and heated some water. The father had cleared above the ledge; he down below, not far from the great fir tree. Then out of nowhere came a rockfall and his father had rolled past him in a cloud of dust, finally coming to a stop a good thirty paces below the place where he was working. Hans had run to him and found him unconscious and as pale as a sheet. With great difficulty, he had dragged him up to the hut where he laid him on some brushwood and splashed his face with water. The father had then come to, had crossed himself and said: "Well, the Devil has *really* sorted me out!"

They noticed that the young man's voice was still shaking with fear. But Nicholas lay quietly, looked at the ceiling and interrupted the story only now and again, saying: "For heaven's sake!" or "God probably willed it so!"

Dorothy passed the following night at his bedside. He was feverish and crossing himself while he dreamt. As the candlelight slowly burnt down, she watched. Despite her anxiety, she loved these hours that delivered him entirely to her care and her eyes guarded him tenderly. She knew all his traits - the scar on the neck and those first silver strands at the temple. She observed how hollow his cheeks had become and how the lines had deepened around the nose and mouth.

When the wick had burnt out, she took her husband's right hand in her cool palms. He accepted it silently and at last seemed to find peace. But suddenly his hand snatched in hers. A shiver seized her and instantly she perceived, in a moment of agonising clarity that flooded her mind and soul: "Heaven and earth are fighting for your husband, Dorothy... And you are there and you can do nothing to help him!"

*   *   *

Klaus soon recovered. The diabolical struggle, however, went on.

During the day he remained impassive and taciturn; he barely ate any more. At night, when he was not sitting up praying on the other side of the room, he lay there motionless and wide-eyed. Dorothy realised with horror that his displays of love were becoming ever more timid and rare, that he sometimes even avoided her and that he was concealing within himself something deep and inexpressible.

Even the birth of a fifth baby girl, on the Feast of the Presentation of the Virgin Mary, failed to bring about the change for which she had hoped. The mother's heart and mind appeared all for the frail little Emma, yet gnawing deeply in her heart was the anguish she felt for her husband. For his part, he lived wholly within himself, wrapped in thought and oblivious to his wife's suffering under the estrangement. Even the child kicking about in the cradle, who possessed the steel-blue eyes of her mother, no longer attracted him.

The winter - longer and with heavier snowfalls than they had had for many years - brought no relief; no purification. Certainly, the following late spring labour brought Nicholas back to earth a little. Yet Dorothy sensed all too clearly that the storm was merely brewing inside him.

On a sunny day in May, when everything was in full bloom and sumptuous, Dorothy was standing at the fount under the lime tree doing the washing.

Straightening herself up a moment, hands on hips to catch her breath, she spied a priest climbing up from the Melchtal gorge. As he got closer, she recognised by the kind eyes in the stern face, Heini am Grund, Klaus' friend and adviser, recently appointed parish priest of Kriens.

He seemed to her like an angel sent by God. She dried her hands and ran towards him. "Easy now! Frau Dorothy!" called the cleric, dabbing his face after the strenuous ascent. But she was already upon him. She looked about quickly to ensure that nobody was observing them and without drawing a breath, pleaded urgently: "Reverend Father, I beg you, help my husband! The Lord and the Evil One are battling for him and I fear that they're tearing him to pieces!"

Reverend Heini, however, already seemed to know everything. "Now is his hour of the dark night, but the day is coming soon which night no longer follows..." he said mysteriously, calming her.

Dorothy summoned Nicholas via Hans, set down before the men in the living room a jug of the best cider, bread, cheese and dried fruit, and before Klaus had time to say to her: "Dorli, be so good and leave us alone a moment...," she had already disappeared.

Upstairs in the children's bedroom, her trembling knees revealed just how much the unexpected appearance of the clerical friend had overwhelmed her. In the cradle, baby Emma kicked her tiny legs and smiled at her mother. She took the babe in her arms and rocked her gently to a soothing, melancholy air:

> "Sleep, baby, sleep.
> Your Father is away at war.
> Your Mother left alone.
> Sleep, baby, sleep.
> Father lying in the snow.
> Mother left alone.
> Sleep, baby, sleep."

As she sang, the haunting words of the priest were ever present: "The day is coming soon which night no longer follows." What could it mean? The peace of heart for which Klaus was struggling in vain? Or, perhaps, death?

And something else tormented her: she felt that God was intruding more and more between she and her husband - and she rebelled against it. She was still young and full of life and very much a woman. She had given herself entirely to Klaus - and now God was disputing her right to him! Before the crucifix, however, her defiance dissolved in holy fear.

In the meantime, night had fallen. The men's voices could still be heard from downstairs but she sensed that things had quietened.

*   *   *

Heini's visit was not without its fruit. Klaus became more settled.

That is not to say that he prayed any less. On the contrary. Scarcely a night passed without him getting up to pray before the large crucifix. Now and again, during the day, Dorothy also found him in the barn or some out-of-the-way place kneeling before a makeshift cross.

One sultry August night, she heard him rise once more. He went out barefoot. The door remained slightly ajar. Dorothy heard him fall to his knees, then everything was quiet again. From time to time a sigh reminded her that he was still there, arms outstretched, face to face with the Crucified; wrestling with God.

Why did he wish to consume himself thus? Why did he have to wear himself out the whole livelong day, fasting into the bargain, and at night stay awake for hours? How she wanted to unburden him! Yet her shoulders were surely too weak for the load!

Eventually he reappeared. Outside, the cock crowed. Shortly afterwards she knew by his quiet breathing that he had fallen asleep. But that did not last long. After a brief slumber, he raised himself up on his elbows and she saw, in the pale early light, that he was looking fixedly towards the door. His eyes seemed to follow an invisible figure that was moving slowly towards him. His lips were forming silent words.

This mute dialogue with the mysterious guest filled her with a paralysing fear. She stretched out her hand beseechingly to the visionary and whispered: "What is it, Klaus?" He came to and turned to her. In his eyes, brimming with mystery, she discerned a gentle reproach.

"What is it?" she repeated insistently.

"Nothing!" he responded, leaning his head against the wall. Yet after some time he began to recount the experience - though really to himself, as if she was not there.

"It seemed to me that someone had entered. Our room appeared as vast and splendid as a castle, full of richly clothed people. Someone was close to me. I didn't see him, but I heard his voice, which filled the castle, saying: "It is he who came to the aid of your son in his distress. Thank him!" Then a most imposing man appeared and went through the palace, dressed in white like a priest at the altar. He laid his two hands around my neck, drew me towards him and thanked me for having come to the aid of his son in his need.

"I was sorely afflicted by this because I knew that I was unworthy of such gratitude. And so I said: "I don't know that I have ever rendered such a service to your son." This man then disappeared and a fair-haired lady approached me. She resembled you and wore, like you on our wedding day, a snow-white gown. She laid both hands on my shoulders, pressed me close and thanked me for having so faithfully assisted her son in his bitter trial. I was shamed by it and declined. Then she too departed... I looked about me and found the son, seated on a throne. He was also clothed in white, but his tunic was sprinkled with blood. He bowed to me and thanked me for having stood by him at the hour of his death... As I lowered my eyes, I saw that I too was wearing a white robe strewn with blood. At that moment, you woke me!"

She loved to hear him tell of such things and had listened attentively, with almost childlike excitement. And yet the leaden weight of her heart told her that this imposing man and this gracious woman and this young man spattered with blood were courting her husband's love, that their irresistible spell was drawing him further and further from her, and that she would struggle in vain against this mighty power.

*   *   *

Dorothy entered her thirty-fifth year. A stranger might have taken her for thirty, even though she had already borne nine children. She still had no grey hairs and her face, though not quite as full, was no less fresh and fine.

Rarely at Flüe had they enjoyed a hay-harvest as plentiful as in this year. The barns were packed to the rafters and the house itself was full of the heady scent of hay. They wondered how they would ever finish the work - not only because the dear Lord was generous with His gifts, but also because the head of the household had his hands full elsewhere. On Monday a messenger called the Councillors to a meeting, which had to settle a dispute between the parish priest and parishioners. Tuesday it was Magistrate von Flüe who had to sit in judgement on a manslaughter charge. Wednesday it was the Captain who had to carry out an inspection... And so went the whole week!

Dorothy often had to meet the onerous demands of an expanding farm and a well-to-do household on her own. Moreover, it was not uncommon for her to stay up till midnight to keep supper warm for her weary husband on his return. At times, late in the evening, he sat down with her on the bench outside or in the parlour, drew out a knife and began carving farm tools or wooden cows for the children. When he had finished, he carefully gathered the shavings in one heap, carried them into the kitchen and cast them onto the hearth. She knew then that he was burdened and it was she who initiated the conversation. If he broke in, she let him speak, sitting quietly and nodding only now and then. In her eyes he read censure, appreciation and praise while her admiring smile was for him the most beautiful earthly reward.

They finally brought in the last loads of hay - just in time - and Klaus should have been gladdened by this and other blessings. A wretched grief, however, weighed on him. On the night of Saints Felix and Regula, long after the evening Angelus had rung over at St. Niklausen, he returned home. When Dorothy put the supper on the table, he endeavoured to smile but his eyes did not respond and betrayed, instead, a deep sadness.

He had scarcely swallowed the first spoonfuls of porridge when he wiped his mouth with the back of his hand and stood up. While Dorothy tidied up the kitchen, he went into the living room and began pacing heavily up and down. The wife felt that he needed to talk something through and so, her work finished, she showed her face at the door and said playfully: "I'll be hearing confessions now, Klaus!" Instead of replying, he pushed a stool towards her and continued his march. Finally, he commenced: "I've thought about it... for months I've thought about it: I can no longer remain Councillor and Judge!" She held her peace.

"What I witnessed today... that's the limit! You know Ueli, the basket weaver, don't you?" Dorothy nodded.

"Well, all right! Do you also know how destitute the old man is! He has a little shack that the torrent will carry away in the next flood, a meadow full of stones twice as big as your kitchen, a goat whose ribs one can count and, as his only earthly consolation, a little daughter chronically ill with consumption! Do you think perhaps that that would be enough misery for the poor beggar? No! During the night, fat Kasper, the wealthiest farmer in the whole valley, actually goes and shifts Ueli's boundary stone in order to enlarge his own property, at Ueli's expense!"

"There are surely wicked people in this world!" Dorothy lamented.

"But wait: that's not the worst of it! The old basket-weaver submits the thing to the court. The facts of the case are crystal-clear... But what happens? They start by dragging out the affair, spinning yarns to the old man. Meanwhile, Kasper isn't sitting idle: to the first Magistrate he promises a barrel of wine, to another he cancels a debt, and to the wife of the third he sends a bale of velvet from Milan. Today was judgement day... I immediately saw that something was wrong. The sentence was decided before the court convened! I thumped the table - in vain! Nobody listened to me. Kasper was cleared of all charges, allegedly for lack of evidence!"

He walked to the window and looked out into the night.

"God in Heaven," he said, gazing up at the stars, "is it possible that Thy Holy Law be treated with such contempt?"

He took a deep breath and sighed heavily: "Ah, to defend Thy Law one would have to be a saint; to have nothing, to be free of everything... "

He turned around and looked into Dorothy's eyes. She sat there, still, hands folded in her lap, looking up at him painfully.

"I'm no saint," he continued, "and I never will be... But I do not want to share in the injustice of others - I cannot uphold that kind of law. In the name of God, what should I do?"

He stopped and waited, as if leaving to her the decision he had already taken, but which he did not wish to carry out without her blessing.

"Well be done with it, Klaus! Be for us again a husband, father and provider - nothing more!"

He reflected for some time, then declared: "You are right Dorothy. I cannot do otherwise. As for the future, God will show me the way!"

A view of Flüeli, situated above the village of Sachseln in central Switzerland. Melchtaler Mountains behind.

The well preserved von Flüe family home, which Klaus himself built for Dorothy and their ten children. In the distance, in the neighbouring hamlet, sits the chapel of St. Nicklausen (middle left).

Living room and kitchen in the von Flüe home.

The idyllic setting of Sachseln on Lake Sarnen. Across the lake, to the right, behind Dorothy's hometown of Sarnen, the mountain chain which includes Pilatus.

PART II

CROWN OF THORNS

As the year 1467 opened, neither Klaus nor Dorothy suspected what a fateful end it held in store for them.

Two weeks before Shrove Tuesday, Hans married. The boys of the neighbourhood sang him a farewell to bachelor days and the girls danced in swirling, airy rings around the smart couple. The adults, on the other hand, were reserved. Nobody knew what the father, Klaus, was pondering behind his low, narrow brow. Nearly everyone realised, however, that amidst the joyous celebration a hidden sorrow was tormenting Dorothy.

Was it not just twenty years ago that they had married? Throughout these years she had matured both with and *through* Klaus. She knew it well. He had led her to the limits of human experience, to the borders of ecstasy and anguish - through a profound and pure understanding they had become deeply united, as if one. Yet for some time now, that innermost part of his being - his soul - had eluded her more and more.

Klaus still wrestled with God! Never before had he fasted as rigorously as this Lent. He partook of no more than a few dried pears, and even that not every day! By the time Easter neared, his hands were cold and his lips pale... Dorothy made motherly reproaches, appealing to his common-sense, but it was useless - he no longer seemed to hear.

The summer passed and Dorothy prepared herself afresh for motherhood, already hindered by her lively burden. The father scarcely noticed, so deeply immersed was he in his thoughts.

Earlier than expected - in late July - the child arrived, a boy. Klaus, who, until then, had refused to give his own name to one of his sons, agreed to allow it this time. The mother thought it proper and was more than pleased, but she discerned by the emotion in his voice that this acquiescence was a legacy, like a last will and testament.

*   *   *

It was nearly a week after the baptism of little Nicholas.

Dorothy had fed the baby and put her youngest to bed. Still a bit pallid, she sat quietly at her spinning wheel. The monotonous work made her doze a little and at first, in the murmur of the wind, she did not hear the door creaking open on its hinges. All of a sudden she stretched out and again took up the slippery thread... Klaus had entered.

He paced up and down the room a few times, then sat himself down at the far end of the bench opposite her. Long and in silence he observed the nimble play of the spindle. Then he rose quickly, went to the window and watched the reddish hue of the evening sky slowly die away.

Without turning to face her, he broke the heavy silence abruptly, almost harshly: "Woman, I have to leave... God wants me!"

She went deathly pale, slowly stood up, staring at him all the while, took a step backwards and leant on the wall. He had turned around and was coming slowly towards her, eyes fastened beseechingly on her lips. Her chin trembled imperceptibly while her pretty head leaned against the hard beam, as if tortured. He was now close to her... Her tearless eyes were burning and her voice was brittle: "It's not possible, Klaus! It cannot be!"

In the weeks that followed, both walked in darkness... At the table, the father said grace, cut the bread crosswise, then stared into his bowl and uttered not a single word. The mother had dark rings around her eyes but none of the children dared to ask what was troubling her. After the meal, Klaus disappeared into the woods and often did not return until far into the night.

On one such homecoming he found his wife crying by the cradle of little Nicholas. Deeply moved, he sat beside her on the edge of the bed and took hold of her slender hand. Looking at the floor, he said with embarrassment: "What's the matter, Dorothy?"

"And our children, what will become of them if you go?" she started, as if continuing an unbroken interior dialogue with him.

"God, Who is taking their father, will Himself be Father to them," he answered.

"And this little mite here?" she said, as the child began to whimper.

"God has already chosen him for His service."

"Are we not bound through the blood of Christ for all eternity?"

"Yes, that we are; and only your free consent can release me - to live alone with God... "

She was silent, lost in her thoughts. Then it burst forth: "But I *cannot* give it! - You took me from my parent's home... You've become everything to me. Brother, father, husband... Everywhere, all I see is you... My sorrow turns to joy when you are sharing it and my joy into bliss if I see it light up your eyes... "

He hid his face in both hands, then said, emphatically: "For you too God will become everything, my child!"

"Oh, God is so far and you so close... It's too much! It's beyond my strength!"

A coughing fit seized the child in the cradle. His mother took

49

him and rocked him gently back to sleep. As the leisurely mooing of cows drifted across the pasture, Klaus went out into the misty dawn.

That evening, Dorothy found her husband kneeling before the cradle, hands joined in front of his mouth. He did not stir. Spellbound, she remained standing in the doorway - but not for long. Her tears overflowed and she called out: "Klaus!"

He gave a start, looked around guardedly, but remained kneeling.

"Klaus! If it's necessary for your happiness, so that you're at peace - I don't want to stand in the way of your happiness... If you cannot be truly happy otherwise; it doesn't matter to me!"

"Oh, woman!" he said. "It's not about *my* happiness, it's about the Will of God. He has bound me; I'm His prisoner and He's leading me where I do not want to go."

"How can I accept that He, Who united us forever, now wants to take you away from me, to have you to Himself?"

"I don't understand it either. I only know that He is the Master and that His love is calling me irresistibly into solitude. Where and why, He alone knows... Ah, yes, if I only knew!"

After an oppressive interval, she went on: "What more can I say? Go on then, go! And God be with you!"

As an after thought, reflecting on it all, she added: "Am I doing it for God, am I doing it for you? I'm just not sure anymore. I only know that I love you more than ever and that I'm saying "yes" out of love for you."

Her face had coloured lightly and her eyes were aglow as once before, when she had given that other, first, sweet "yes."

Eyes riveted on her, Klaus slowly picked himself up. He raised his calloused hand as if wanting to caress her locks but left off midway through the gesture and let the hand fall - in renunciation.

She perceived the movement and had offered her neck in return. The warm touch she longed for, however, did not arrive.

The "adieu" had commenced. She threw herself on her knees before the bed, buried her head in the sheets and sobbed bitterly...

*   *   *

The following three days weighed heavily on the von Flüe household. The father disclosed his intentions to his eldest children and counted the ready cash with them. The mother cut out a long, strange garment. The young girls burst into tears whenever they looked at each other or encountered their mother.

On the eve of St. Gallus - a clear, mild autumn day with a soft wind, so that one could have counted the fir trees on the Sachseln mountain above - Klaus made one final round of his property with Walter. Dorothy stood on the doorstep and looked after them. She watched him pat the heads of the cows at the drinking trough and with a robust step, stride through the meadows, pointing out this and that boundary stone to his son until, finally, the woods engulfed them.

Klaus and Dorothy passed their last night together in prayer. When the morning star appeared in the blue notch between Pilatus and the Stanserhorn, husband and wife bid farewell to each other forever.

The first cock had just crowed as Dorothy, candle in hand, entered the girls room. She had no need to wake anyone. Verena sat crying on her bed. The slender Dorli, almost a young woman now, came to her and embraced her ardently. The mother gently freed herself from her cool arms, said to the little ones: "Dress yourselves warmly, children!" and went into the boys room. They were all still sleeping, or pretending to be. In the light of the flame, she contemplated a moment the full, red cheeks of the young ones and the gaunt, virile features of the older. "Poor little orphans," she thought, "and in their father's lifetime!" Then, as was her custom, she called firmly: "Praised be Jesus Christ!" Walter jumped up promptly and let his mother sign a cross on his forehead, mouth and breast. The others followed suit, one by one. No one said a word.

Soon afterwards, the whole family gathered silently in the living room. On the bench against the wall, next to the door, sat Uncle Peter, sullenly carving a small piece of wood. Opposite him by the hearth, chin propped on his walking stick, crouched the lifeless figure of Klaus' frail, sunken-eyed father. The children were standing in front of the window, a little apart from Hans and his young wife. In the corner, near the door to the parent's bedroom, the servants waited... Dorothy was last to arrive, babe in arm. Everyone was quiet, timorously following the soft, muffled steps which went back and forth over in the parental chamber.

Each held their breath when the sound left off for a moment. There was a creaking noise and the father appeared in the doorway. He wore a coarse, brown habit over his bare body and held a staff in his right hand. He looked at them, one after the other, engraving their features in his memory forever.

"My children!" he began, "God is calling me. You cannot comprehend it now, and neither can I... but I know He's calling me. From this moment on, He Himself will be your Father and Protector. Fear Him and honour your mother!"

Then he blessed each of them, from youngest to oldest, with a small cross on the forehead. Walter knelt down. Peter silently pressed the hand while his aged father grasped it and shook it, speechless. The daughters sobbed.

To Dorothy he said nothing, nor did he bless her, for fear of liberating too much emotion and weakening their resolve. Instead, he secretly traced a tiny cross on her heart.

They accompanied him to the door - he had insisted that they should go no further; there he parted with them and walked away into the clear night. At the hedge he turned one last time and called with trembling voice: "May God bless you!" Then he strode off, his steps soon devoured by the roar of the Melchaa...

Somewhere a dog howled. The ghostly call of a barn owl rang out in the forest. Dorothy shivered.

*　　　*　　　*

For three days it had snowed continuously. So extravagant was this first fall that the house was cut-off from the world. Only the route to the neighbouring residence, where Hans had taken his wife the previous spring was more or less passable. In any event, who wanted to open-up the path down into the valley? For what purpose? Since that momentous St. Gallus' day, no one had left the Flüeli domain and no one had called there.

On the eve of All Souls, Peter was in the living-room carving handsome wooden dolls for the girls. Verena was seated at the spinning wheel where her nimble fingers slipped and wound fine grey threads in steady rhythm. Dorli was busy crocheting.

The silence in the warm room would have been complete but for the hum of the wheel and the regular tread that issued from the mother's bedroom. Indeed, it was this step that commanded the silence and stifled each budding word.

The door opened. It was Hans. There were still snowflakes in his new, scrawny beard and he appeared anxious. They quietly welcomed him while he looked about as though searching for someone.

"Good evening," he offered after his brief survey. Then he sat down on the wall-bench, behind the table, and watched his uncle work. Soon the dull sound in the neighbouring room caught his attention. He looked across at the door and asked, thoughtfully: "Is it always thus?" Dorli began to cry.

"Ever since it started snowing it's been like that," Verena confirmed. "Poor Mother! She doesn't know where Father is and probably imagines that he's under the snow somewhere... God knows where he can be - perhaps starving, frozen... dead?"

"It's more than two weeks since he left," Hans remarked to

himself, "and nobody has seen him!"

After brooding for some time, he ventured: "Mother never comes near you?"

Dorli wept. Verena caressed her dainty hand. "Less and less," she answered. "She only comes to give a few instructions and often goes off to the corner of the garden where Father planted a sapling from The Ranft before he left. I saw her today from the window. She shook the snow from its branches and looked at it for a long time... "

"I ask myself how that will all turn out?" said Uncle Peter, who until then had carried on carving as if the discussion did not concern him.

"Who knows... And the worst is that people are gossiping; everybody's talking about us," said Hans. "Yesterday, down in Sarnen, the butcher's boy had the cheek to ask me if it was true that Father and Mother couldn't get along together! You can imagine that I shut the impertinent fellow's mouth; but you'd need a thousand hands to silence all the wagging tongues."

"People don't even want to understand. And if you don't give them an explanation, they invent one themselves," decreed Peter.

"Just who *can* understand?" sighed Hans. "Anyway, no explanation would satisfy them."

There was a hush - save for the mother's footsteps.

"Yesterday," said Verena finally, "when Mother came into the kitchen, Ruedi asked her: 'Mummy, why isn't papa coming home for so long?' And looking at Ruedi and me, she said, 'I don't know, my child! I don't know any more than you! I only know that what God wants is good and what your Father is doing is good... We'll probably understand it later'."

"Later - or never!" added Peter caustically.

"Poor Mother!" said Hans. "Have you noticed that every evening she places a night light on the windowsill? Obviously so that Father can find the house again, if he were to come home... I see it from the stable."

At that moment they heard the bolt shift and the door opened.

Dorothy stood a moment in the black opening, to accustom her eyes to the light. Dorli ran to her and hid her tear-stained face in her breast.

The mother was pale, her forehead lined with beads of perspiration. Her upright composure betrayed effort. Yet she smiled when she recognised Hans, who had risen and was approaching her.

"How is your wife?" she asked.

"Very well, thank you Mother! We hope our little one will arrive before Epiphany - God willing!" She assented absently.

After sizing up Verena's distaff, bound in flaxen fibres, she said: "Child, that's enough work now! You're worn out!" Then to Peter: "And your foot, how is it? Come into the kitchen and I'll change your bandage."

Peter had in fact cut himself with the scythe while reaping and suffered from a festering wound. He rose and followed her. She had not reached the door before turning round once more: "Pray for your poor Father in the snow! Good night!" she said.

And with that, she quickly turned away and passed into the darkness.

*   *   *

Peter was a passionate hunter. In early November, when he heard that a family of bears had been sighted high in the Melchtal, neither his stiff leg nor his sore foot could keep him from whetting his knife and spear and searching out his hunting companions.

The little troop were away four days. Towards evening - the wind howling and the Melchaa roaring - they returned home tired and drenched. In the kitchen Dorothy relieved Peter of his bag. She saw from the look on his face that he had returned empty-handed and, smiling, she joked: "Can I make you that new doublet out of bearskin, Peter?" The hunter, however, was in no mood for pleasantries and muttered something to himself.

"Is it your foot that pains you?" she asked anxiously.

"No, not that!" he retorted. "But I have a message for you Dorothy." He opened the door to the parlour, showed her in, followed behind and bolted the door.

Searching his features, she sat down on the edge of the chest under the window while he, striding about agitated and undecided, drew out a hunting-knife and began stroking the tip. Her pulse quickened.

"We found him!" he declared all of a sudden. "We've found your husband!"

Dorothy closed her eyes and leant against the casement.

"Yesterday evening, we reached our pasture up at Klisterli; we wanted to spend the night there. I went to open the door and found it ajar. I carefully felt my way in and saw, in the semi-darkness, someone kneeling on the ground. He didn't see me; he didn't hear me... I walked towards him, looked him in the face and... it was Klaus!"

She had risen and was advancing on him: "What's the matter with you, Peter? You've lost your head! Seeing that my husband is in Alsace. Or else he could've died and you've met his ghost?"

"No, no! It's him - in the flesh... Admittedly, he looks a wreck. Beard and hair matted, the cheeks haggard and bloodless, the lips cracked... "

"My poor Klaus!" sighed Dorothy. "Does it all really have to be like this, Peter?"

"Who knows," he growled. "In any case, I don't like the whole business one bit!"

"But why then isn't he in Alsace? That was his destination - to join a community of the Friends of God in Strasbourg!"

"Heaven only knows! He merely told us that after having left here he went as far as the Jura. On the first night, he said he had a dream in which he was ordered to return home. 'Where God wants me to settle is to this day still a mystery to me,' he said."

"Dear Lord, if he could at last only find his place of peace!" she lamented and began to weep quietly. Peter, still holding his knife, jabbed at a log that lay on the windowsill. He dared not look at her.

"But that's not the worst of it," he said, pursuing his thoughts out loud. "The worst is that he eats hardly anything, or perhaps even nothing at all. I wanted to leave him my ham, but he stubbornly refused. Afterwards I beseeched him not to destroy himself, and would you believe that he said to me: 'If God has kept me until now, He will continue to keep me!' That's all I was able to get out of him."

*   *   *

At the end of March, Walter brought news that neighbours had wanted to visit their father up on the alpine pasture but had not found him. Evidently, he had disappeared. But to where, nobody knew. Some thought he had gone over to the Engelberg valley, others - the boy was uneasy; his stomach tightened - others were saying that he had fallen somewhere and that the snow had covered him.

By mid-April, exceptionally warm spring sunshine had melted nearly all the snow. One day, Erny Rohrer, a childhood friend of Klaus, arrived at Flüe. He asked to see the mistress of the house and wanted to speak to her in private. Dorothy conducted the farmer into the parlour where he told her: "It's Klaus who sent me... He's down below, in The Ranft, several hundred paces from here!"

A burst of crimson filled the woman's face. She opened her mouth, but the word remained stuck in her throat. The man read in her eyes that she knew not whether to fear or to hope.

"He said," he continued, "that God has pointed out to him this gorge as his earthly home, that he wants to build a hermitage there and he'd like Peter and Walter to help him!"

Dorothy lowered her eyes and fought against her swelling indignation. So Klaus was calling his brother and his son; but for her, his wife - not a word! No invitation to come down to see him, to care for him. And why, of all places - if he truly had to live in solitude - did he have to settle right outside her door, like a beggar?

Erny guessed what was going on inside her. "Console yourself, woman," he said, "since he's now so close, he will certainly not leave you completely alone."

"Don't you believe it!" said Dorothy in a flash of pride. "What Klaus undertakes he carries through relentlessly to the end, and what he does he doesn't do by halves! This house no longer exists for him... for him, I am dead!"

She said this not without a certain ferocity. At once, however, she regained her composure: "Tell my husband that I will also send him Hans, since his house will soon be finished."

"And tell him," she added, lowering her eyes once more, "tell him that he is in my thoughts... always!"

Commencing the following day and for the next month and a half, the three men descended each morning to The Ranft and only returned late in the evening. Peter hardly spoke during this time; Hans went home again immediately after the work. So every evening, Dorothy took Walter aside and questioned him about his father's condition.

"Father always asks after you Mother," said the young man. "He wants to know if you've not suffered too much from his leaving, if little Nicholas wakes you often and whether you're getting by on the money."

The mother smiled. Yet, always, she waited for more: for a call from him.

Finally, late one afternoon, when the hermitage was finished and as Dorothy's desire was growing with each new day, Walter reported to her: "Listen Mother: Father says to tell you that he still cannot see you, God does not yet permit it."

The colour drained from Dorothy's face. She had thought herself so close to her goal and now, again, her hope dissolved. She turned the message over in her mind. The words "not yet..." recurred to her again and again. "So perhaps, then - later!" she thought.

At the very start of the work at Ranft, Walter had brought his father a full bag of choice dried pears. Two weeks later, however, the bag had come back untouched. When Hans asked the father, who always kept out of the way during mealtimes, if he eat nothing, he had simply answered: "God knows!" Nothing more was gleaned from him.

One day as Dorothy was kneeling in her sticky, black garden soil planting lettuce beds, Frau Omlin, the portly wife of the Magistrate, passed by the hedge puffing and blowing. She stepped closer and looked a while at the gardener.

"I wager that the lettuce will be beautiful, in this good soil," she began unexpectedly, by way of introduction.

Dorothy picked herself up: "Ah, hello Frau Omlin!"

"And how is Herr Klaus?" asked the woman furtively, looking Dorothy straight in the eye.

The latter examined her seedlings as if counting their little heads, and responded without looking up: "Oh, as well as can be expected down there."

"Have you already been to see him?"

"No."

"But you'll certainly send him something to eat?"

"No."

"Surely he won't have to live on roots and berries just a few minutes from your very door?"

Dorothy did not answer.

"But what is he living on then, if nobody takes him anything?"

"God knows!" Dorothy shot back equivocally and looked to

continue her chore.

"You know, there are *some* people who claim that he's fed by angels," persisted the neighbour undeterred.

Dorothy flared up: "Nobody, neither he nor anyone of us has ever claimed that!"

"Others say that it's all just a fraud!" added the corpulent one in a taunting voice charged with derision.

Dorothy took up her basket. "Good evening, Frau Omlin!" she said brusquely, then turned and went inside.

The children reported similar rumours. "Mad" Simon said that von Flüe had been a good neighbour; *but*, that he no longer ate, like the angels in Heaven, he, Simon, was not having it. He would swallow a broom whole, if Klaus' wife was not supplying him with food and drink by night!

After that, Dorothy hardly dared to venture out. Now it was she who prayed half the night before the large crucifix.

She was preparing the family meal one evening when little Ruedi ran in, tugged her apron and demanded: "Mother, what do they want, those men, who wait at the edge of the forest all day? They always look down into The Ranft so nastily... If they want to do something to papa, then I'm going to bash their heads!"

"Stop it Ruedi!" the mother protested, "they're not nasty and will do nothing to papa. - Perhaps they're watching out for someone who wants to be nasty to him?" she added reassuringly.

The poor woman knew that the men who had stood guard night and day for nearly a month, were sent by the government itself. Talk of Klaus' miraculous fast had so excited the people that the rulers had deemed it necessary to clear up the mystery, thus organising a relentless watch of every approach to Ranft.

Not long afterwards, beaming with delight and breathless, Ruedi again ran to his mother and called out to her: "Mama, the nasty men have gone!"

Indeed, they had gone, and they never came back...

Dorothy had always known that her husband was the object of

a miraculous grace. Would all the people now also believe it - believe it as firmly as she?

*   *   *

Easter fell early in the second year following the father's departure, as did the first warm weather and the first greenery in the countryside.

Frau Dorothy was feeling weary after the biting winter. In the afternoon, she sat gladly on the bench outside the house, carding wool and savouring the last rays of sunlight.

It was thus that on the Thursday after the Easter rogation solemnities, having swept the kitchen, she retired to her favourite spot for a short rest. It then occurred to her that twenty-three years ago she had celebrated her betrothal to Klaus.

No one had thought of it... or perhaps had not wanted to remind her that the happiness of times past had been shattered.

Words and images welled up in her heart. She still heard the warm tone of his voice when he called her name for the first time. Tears that she had shed on her wedding night, when left alone with him, now seemed to her sweet and joyful. She saw again, too, that glow in his eyes as she laid the first born son in his arms...

Would that her love could bring him back! Had God no pity for her? Was Klaus not the victim of an unfortunate mistake? Perhaps, in the silence, his soul would again find peace and bring him to his senses. What was the point of such a sacrifice, tearing apart those who belonged together?

She was so immersed in these thoughts, that she did not notice the strange cortege coming up from The Ranft. At the head, on a shaggy and obviously stubborn mule, rode a priest in a white surplice. Behind him came a bishop astride his steed, wearing a red hat and a dark cloak, under which flashed the hem of a likewise red soutane. Then a servant led a horse heavily loaded with chests and leather bags. At a distance followed some Councillors in the colours of Lucerne and Nidwalden and, lastly, judges and priests in black.

When Dorothy eventually looked up and set eyes on the rider, she rose reverently, hoping these distinguished lords might pass by her garden on the way down to Sachseln. But no! The bishop rode straight towards her!

She dropped her wool and stood motionless in front of her little bench. The dignitary - a tall, refined gentleman - had already swung himself out of the saddle and was approaching her with a sprightly step. He bent down to pick up the wool and then offered her his ring.

Dorothy had knelt down and pressed her lips devoutly to the sparkling red stone. The bishop signed a cross on her forehead and helped her up again.

"Are you the wife of the blessed man there below?" he asked her.

Dorothy felt herself blush. It was, after all, the first time she had spoken to a Prince of the Church; and on top of that he called her husband blessed! Still, she controlled her emotion: "If you will pardon my saying so: Yes, my Lord."

The prelate questioned her no further; but his look, at once fatherly and searching, settled on her eyes. She sensed that she could hide nothing from him; that he understood everything and pardoned, too, all the contradictions which abounded in her, even to rebellion.

"God is greater than our heart!" he said, as if for her alone. And then, stressing each word: "Blessed those who mourn, for they shall be comforted."

He obliged her to sit down and without fuss took a seat beside her, notwithstanding the gentlemen who looked on curiously over the hedge.

"God," he commenced, "has clearly both accepted and blessed your sacrifice. As a pledge of His blessing, He has given your husband the rare, perhaps unique gift of total abstention from food and drink. I have examined him in this matter and will vouch for the fact that for two years, he has eaten nothing and drunk nothing."

Conflicting emotions erupted violently within Dorothy and her heart began to pound impetuously. She had resisted, with all the passion of her great human love, the divine call that snatched her husband from her. Ever since he left, she had struggled daily to submit her wilful heart to the Divine Will... And now she learnt - it seemed to her as if from the mouth of God Himself - that the sacrifice of her love, all the tears, all her humiliations and despair were fruitful for her husband and his mission!

Another heartfelt burden also lifted from her. Certainly, she had never doubted the miracle that God had worked in her husband; but what torment she had endured, having to listen to the idle gossip of the people and looking on helplessly as day and night he was kept under surveillance, like a criminal.

She felt like someone who had long walked in darkness and then suddenly emerged into the light: she was dazzled...

The bishop could see her reeling and held his peace for a moment. When her cheeks had regained their colour, he stood up and said: "God Himself has desired your sacrifice, Madame! It will not go unrewarded!" Dorothy seized the consecrated hand and pressed it to her mouth. "With the help of the Almighty, your husband will accomplish still greater things yet!" he said, blessed her once more and resumed his journey.

The sun also moved on, casting a lofty, red glow above the snowy peaks. In the clearness of the twilight, an eagle slowly turned...

*   *   *

After government and bishop had recognised the miraculous fast, Dorothy waited each day for an invitation from Ranft. It did not come. She learnt only that her husband had suffered for forty days from the two bits of bread the bishop had obliged him to eat during his visit.

At last, on the Feast of the Visitation, Walter returned excited from morning Mass. Outside the church in Sachseln he had met his father, who had taken him aside and whispered in his ear: "Tell Mother, that she should come down to me this afternoon with you children... Since today is a feast of the Mother of God!"

Dorothy could scarcely believe it. She ran first to the garden, to cut some roses. Then she fetched from her chest the silk dress she had inherited on the death of her mother, turned towards the crucifix and gave thanks. She washed and scrubbed the children and entered into such great preparations that she very nearly left the gruel to burn.

After vespers in Sachseln, the mother gathered her children around her. Hans had excused himself. Verena had married since Christmas and was expecting her first child. Walter, who saw his father nearly every day, was visiting his fiancée. Nicholas and Emma, the youngest, had been entrusted to Hans' wife.

So, on the descent to Ranft, Dorothy tallied only five small heads. The two boys, Ruedi and Heini, took the lead - veritable little savages, chasing after butterflies and decapitating white hemlocks. Then came the two girls, already womanly and reserved: Dorli, the austere beauty, leading by the hand the delicate Margaret. Both were picking blue bellflowers for their father. On her mother's hand toddled little Anna.

Dorothy was in a strange mood. Overcome by the heady scent of blossoms, she was now ascending to the altar on her wedding day; now escorting her husband to the grave - joyous and comfortless by turns, emotions churning in her heart like storm-clouds in a capricious sky.

Through the light foliage of the beeches she saw, for the first time, the white chapel with its straw-coloured shingle roof and, resting against it, the wooden-brown hermitage. But her eyes searched for something more! She looked and looked - until, finally, a little further on, at the shady edge of the woods, she found a man seated on a pile of stones. He held a heavy rosary in his hands and his eyes followed a buzzard that was spiralling upwards into the blue above the forest. Klaus! For a second, her heart stopped. She propped herself on little Anna's shoulder. That hermit there with the dishevelled beard and the long habit she had woven with her own hands - that was her Nicholas!

The boys had hurried on ahead and were leading their father towards her. Dorothy could no longer contain herself and started running.

"Nicholas!" she stammered when she finally stood before him.

"Dorothy!" he returned quietly and looked at her. After a short silence he said simply: "Come and see where I live!"

He walked beside her towards the chapel, asking after her health and for news of little Nicholas, last years harvest, the new roof Walter had put on the old barn... She could only answer "yes" or "no," "good" or "bad," her eyes fixed firmly on the ground.

Together they entered the chapel, where at first Dorothy saw only the venerable wooden crucifix over the altar. She instructed Dorli to lay down the bellflowers and her roses at the feet of the Saviour and knelt down on the stone slab next to Klaus. When they were all together, the father, with strong voice, commenced the Pater Noster. Everyone joined in, as they were accustomed to doing at home... *"Fiat voluntas tua!*... Thy will be done!"... said Klaus firmly. Dorothy's voice wavered.

He then lead his family out to the small side door and the stairs which climbed up to his cell. When she entered and looked about, Dorothy's heart pounded. The room was so low that her husband's hair brushed the ceiling, and so narrow that a tall man with outstretched arms could have touched both walls. In it they saw nothing other than a bench, two footstools, a smooth, flat stone and a worn-out blanket.

"Where's your bed, papa?" asked the six-year old Margaret curiously.

"There, child!" the father replied smiling, and pointed his finger at the floor-boards and the smooth stone. Dorothy masked her dismay.

Anna now also wanted to know where the father ate. Klaus guided her to a peephole through which one saw the interior of the chapel and the altar. "Look," he explained, "when the priest there below raises the Holy Eucharist, then your father has eaten and drunk!" The child was unable to grasp how a man as big as her father could live on such a small Host. The mother smiled in sympathy.

After the girls had explored the wooden walls, the boys had lifted the heavy stone up to their knees several times and the eyes of the parents had met timidly two or three times, Klaus invited them to sit down.

The mother took one stool and Dorli the other, the two little girls heaved themselves up onto the bench and the two boys, back to back, made do with the stone.

The father leant on a wall-beam and began in his deep, warm voice: "Since today is the Feast of Our Lady - children! - I want to tell you something about the Holy Virgin Mary, Queen of Heaven and Earth, Who was chosen by Divine Love to be the Mother of Our Lord and Saviour... When from eternity God took this decision, He at once wrapped His love and grace around Her to save Her from all sin."

Dorothy still dared not look directly at him. Instead, she followed his huge, gnarled hands, now lucent in their thinness, which slowly and solemnly punctuated his words.

"This is why She is pure, gentle and immaculate. The power of the Almighty has overshadowed and filled Her with the Holy Ghost."

He spoke so familiarly that Dorothy raised her eyes.

A strange, ecstatic chill gripped her. Was it that look of heavenly radiance, or the well-formed mouth; was it that bold sweep of the nose, or the wild hair that shook her so? She did not know but felt only that something extraordinary had happened to him, something at once enchanting and overbearing; which enticed her and yet kept her imperiously at arms length.

"The generous Creator, Who embraces all the Heavens," the hermit continued, "dwelt in Mary as a little child, and in and through Her He gave us that same tender body He now gives to us, in His undivided Godhead, as food!" He was in ecstasy!... A moment passed until he again realised that he had his family before him.

In the meantime, evening was falling; it had become dark and sultry in the cramped cell.

Klaus blessed them and accompanied them to the edge of the forest. The children scurried ahead; father and mother lagging a little behind.

"Is the sacrifice accomplished, Dorothy?" he uttered unexpectedly, breaking the stillness.

"I struggle with it every day!" she replied. "If I could only offer it to God without reserve! But He knows that the last ounce of my being yearns for Him... that I'm surrendering myself entirely to His Will!"

Klaus remained silent.

When they had arrived on the fringe of the woods, she looked at him and said: "I think I could find peace, simply knowing that you are happy... "

He perceived the underlying question but evaded it: "Woman, it's not a matter of my *happiness*, but of our *obedience*. And we have to strive for this obedience - daily!"

"Be patient with me!" she implored. "Bear with my hesitation and my misery and my tears - until I'm able to stand purified with you before God."

"Good night, Dorothy!" he concluded suddenly.

"Good night, Klaus," she said in turn, and with hurried steps climbed back home.

Deep in thought, his eyes followed her for some time; then he turned back to the chapel, where he passed the rest of the night in prayer.

*   *   *

It was a cool May morning. After a night of fierce rain, the whole countryside was refreshed and bright. Dorothy was in the kitchen preparing some pigswill.

Someone knocked timidly at the door and two young lads stuck their heads in: "Good morning, Frau Dorothy," said the oldest. "We have a message from our priest!"

Frau Dorothy lifted the cauldron from the fire and invited the boys into the room. "Welcome!" she said. "And what do you have to pass on?"

"The parish priest of Kerns sent us to tell you that he's saying Mass down at Ranft and would you like to come?" said the younger one boldly.

Dorothy swept into her bedroom, folded her apron and stroked her forehead and cheeks with her hands. She tied a cheerful, blue scarf around her head and called through the window to little Nicholas who was cutting some wood: "Come, my child, come! We're going to Father!"

The last word virtually stuck in her throat and she had to press both hands on her heart. It still beat faster whenever she had to meet her husband unexpectedly.

In passing, she took a mixed bunch of wildflowers from the table, then motioned to the three boys and led them out into the rain-soaked and radiant morning.

Young Nicholas clung to her free arm and naturally wanted to know a thousand things: Why they were going down today? Whether another bishop with a red pom-pom was at papa's house? Who exactly were the two boys? And many such weighty details besides.

Dorothy answered all the questions distractedly. Her happy eyes were delighting in the glitter of raindrops which hung from every blade of grass and leaf; her ears attuned to the eternal, melancholy chant of the Melchaa, which spoke of transience and farewells - like an old, familiar hymn that after long years one suddenly understands... A stabbing pain at once revived her deep and bloodied wound.

Outside the Ranft chapel a lordly gentleman was waiting, beard trimmed in the German style and the wine-coloured, fur-lined coat undone. When he saw her he came forward and bowed courteously. He introduced himself and escorted her to a bench against the outer wall of the cell.

While inside the priest was donning his holy vestments and Nicholas - as well as his clumsy young hands could - was arranging his mother's flowers before the image of Our Lady, the gentleman calmly questioned Dorothy about her husband. He wanted to know everything: when he had left her, his age at the time, how she felt about it and all manner of things.

The prying questions troubled her. But what really disconcerted was a familiar step she heard pacing up and down behind the cold, damp wall on which they were leaning. She hardly lent an ear to the visitor's nonchalant, self-satisfied chatter, waiting only for the liberating toll of the chapel bell! When at last it called them to the Holy Sacrifice, Dorothy got up hastily and took her leave from the squire... No sooner had she knelt down in the last pew and closed her eyes to better recollect herself, than she heard above her, up in the wall, the rattle of a little window being gently pushed open. She knew it was Klaus and felt his look touch her. Slender fingers quickly masked a sudden, surprising blush.

"Introibo ad altare Dei... I will go into the altar of God"... the priest began the celebration of Mass.

Slowly, the waves of emotion within her subsided. She looked up at the Crucified and knew, with a wifely intuition, that their eyes met there, as one, in Him. "If ever you are missing me," he had once said to her, "then look for me in the wound of the Sacred Heart!" She now buried herself in that divine scar and in truth his promise was realised: it seemed to her as if their two souls touched - fleetingly, no longer than a heartbeat; yet how deeply and fervently.

"Suscipe, Sancte Pater..." The priest elevated the paten. How she loved this sacrificial gesture of anointed hands! She perceived that their common destiny was being realised before her. It was not a Host but two hearts that lay there on the precious gold plate: one still bleeding, the other already transfigured and at peace!

When the celebrant raised the chalice, a sunbeam caught the sacred vessel which suddenly blazed as if fire from Heaven had consumed the double offering.

"It is done!" she sighed.

The Holy Mass was finished... Above her, a bolt creaked and a cheerful voice called down into the little church: "May God grant you a fine morning, my dear friends and visitors!" A murmur acknowledged the greeting.

Dorothy took young Nicholas by the hand and without a backwards glance, went home.

The Ranft gorge. Middle left, Klaus' hermitage and adjoining chapel. In the foreground, the lower-Ranft chapel (built 1501) beside the Melchaa torrent. In the background, upper right, mount Pilatus.

St. Nicholas von Flüe.
(The earliest picture, painted five years after his death.)

The hermitage and chapel.

Brother Klaus' cell. 3.10 metres long, 2.80 metres wide and 1.80 metres high. To the right, the window at which he knelt to follow Holy Mass in the chapel below. Klaus slept on the bare floor and during the severe winters used only an old blanket.

PART III

CROWN OF
PRECIOUS STONES

Never, as far as Dorothy could recall, had the fires burned so frequently on the hills nor the tocsin so often raised the alarm as in this year. Men were literally called to arms in the middle of their work. And so the women themselves had strained under the ploughs and in the evenings consumed themselves with worry about father, brother or husband who fought somewhere far away.

A proud and powerful enemy, Charles the Bold, Duke of Burgundy, threatened the country.

On the eleventh of June, Dorothy was hanging out her washing in the meadow when young Klaus came running from the forest. "Mother," he cried from a distance, "look at the cloud of smoke on Pilatus!"

She turned and saw yonder a dark column of smoke climbing up into the blue sky. War! It flashed through her mind that her two eldest would have to leave and Verena's husband too.

Around midday, the Sarnen bell began to sound. Giswil's responded, then Kern's and soon the whole valley resounded with furious ringing.

Early in the afternoon, Hans appeared in the kitchen in full armour, squeezed his mother's hand and scurried off in the direction of Ranft. Walter came a little later. He was exuberant and declared: "Mother, now it's off to a real battle, as I've long desired!" Despite her anxiety, Dorothy felt proud of her valiant young officer. She took a small rose from a bouquet and stuck it in his helmet. "May God be with you lad!" she called after him as he strode away urgently towards The Ranft.

Two weeks passed. News of the war was conflicting. Then, on Sunday after Mass, they learnt of the great victory at Murten. It spread like wildfire. They had massacred the Burgundians to a man, asserted one; they had seized the Duke's treasure and thrown the lot into the lake, assured the other - at which the little boys made merry with a rhyme:

"Charles the Bold, wet and cold!
Lost his army, lost his gold!"

In the evening, all the bells rang joyfully anew while fires of victory blazed on the mountains.

On Tuesday evening, Dorothy heard the noise of horses hooves in front of the house. She went to open: a cavalryman approached her, leading his mount by the reins. He greeted her and asked if he was at the home of Brother Klaus. She concurred as a dreadful premonition flashed before her. The guest was shown into the chamber near the entrance.

"Your two sons are safe and well and send their regards!" said the sergeant upon entering. "But they are still occupied with dividing up the enormous booty and will probably not be back till the end of the week."

Dorothy heaved a sigh of relief, had the young man sit down

and took a place beside him.

"Unfortunately, I also have some sad news for you," he said quietly after a pause. "Ueli Uchsberg from Englerts on the Altsellen, your daughter Verena's husband, has fallen on the field of honour defending the Fatherland."

He stood up again, made a long, respectful military salute and left her alone.

The following day was sultry. Threatening clouds loomed. Towards evening, as thunder and lightning mounted, the first summer storm broke.

At the height of the downpour, there was a knock at the door. Dorothy dropped the wood she was holding and opened... In the driving rain, drenched and pale, stood Verena and her brother-in-law, his head wrapped in a blood-soaked bandage. "Dear Lord! In this weather!" Dorothy cried out. The young woman threw her arms around her neck. "Oh Mother, Mother!" she wailed.

"Come in, my poor child," said the mother leading her towards the fire. She brought forward two stools and carefully removed the man's beret. "I already know everything," she whispered, ridding the daughter of her sodden scarf.

"My God! Ueli's dead! Only two weeks ago, as he went off, he was joking and kissing me... And now, now he's lying cold and lifeless under a pile of bodies... They only brought me back his battered helmet!"

Margaret and the long-legged Heini, meanwhile, had drawn near. Without a word, Margaret laid her hands on the shoulders of her older sister; Heini clasped her hand and sat close to her on the bench. Her mother rekindled the fire in order to warm some milk.

"Where and how did he fall?" asked Heini awkwardly, attempting to ease the oppressive mood.

The wounded - twin brother of the dead man - poked about in the fire with his baton and slowly began to explain:

"Only a week ago we marched into Berne. There was great

noise and excitement. Everybody was at the window or down in the street. There were processions, lines of wagons, weapons and soldiers arriving from everywhere.

"After a short rest, we had to set off again and arrived the same night, in constant rain! in an endless forest... where the army assembled. You should've been there: a pitch-black night and swarming like an ant-thill besides!

"On Friday night came orders to move on. We marched in long, silent columns through the forest sludge. I remember Ueli said to me 'There's some pretty wood!' and pointed towards the great beeches with the end of his pike...

"From midnight, the rain came again. The forest paths became streams. We had to wade ankle deep in the water. There were orders, counter-orders - and so it went till dawn!

"When the rain eased off a bit, we got out of the forest... and then, you wouldn't believe it! A gusty wind scattered the clouds and the sun appeared! The whole countryside shone and everything glittered: the spears - thousands upon thousands - the swords of the cavaliers, helmets, armour... On the right we saw Murten, savagely bombed and still half-covered with clouds of smoke; to the left, on a pointy hill, we saw the Burgundian encampment - a mass of colour and noise... there was plenty going on up there! Cavaliers were mounting, columns of archers taking up position, horses neighing and rearing - not to mention the thunder of the cannonade in front of the city!

"When we knelt down in the wet grass to commend ourselves to the Ten Thousand martyrs, rifles and canons had already struck up a tune opposite us - Boom! Boom!

" 'God be with you!' Ueli said to me - they were his last words.

"Then it started! Our troop attacked a large canon that was firing straight at us. The first shot was aimed too high and passed over our heads. We started trotting forward. In front of us, the Burgundy men madly stuffed the steaming muzzles with powder and cannonballs - we saw it all clearly!

"We got to within twenty paces of the entrenchment - all of a sudden, I see the canon flare up! 'Lord,' I'm thinking, 'have mercy on us!' A whistle and - Ueli fell heavily, beside me... It had torn him to pieces!

"I could only remove his helmet and then... Charge! Damn them all! I avenged him, poor Ueli!

"But suddenly, in the middle of the fight around this canon, I felt a mighty blow on the helmet. I fell and don't recall anything after that."

During the account, as the wounded roused himself more and more, Verena had been assailed by a fit of the shivers.

"You're not well, my poor girl!" said the mother placing a bowl of boiling milk in her trembling hands. "Come to bed! And you," she said to Margaret, "look after Oswald. Dress his wound and prepare a bed for him!"

For several hours Dorothy watch by the bed of the young widow. In the quiet, Verena dozed. When the church clock over at St. Niklausen struck eleven, she emerged from her torpor and said weakly: "Mother, you know how much I loved Ueli! I can hardly believe that I'll never see his eyes again, never again hear his voice..." The mother took the daughter's feverish hand in hers. "Mother," she carried on still softer, "I think now - only now - can I see how cruelly you must have suffered when father went away. Death has taken my husband; one can do nothing about it. But yours is still alive, and yet for you he is dead!"

"Never mind that, little one!" Dorothy said quickly. "The Lord has given me strength to carry this cross; he will give it to you too." Then she added: "Tomorrow you will go to your father. He'll know how to comfort you better than me."

She stood up and tucked in her grown-up daughter - as when she was a child and would happily let her mother pull the covers up under her chin - smoothed the sweaty hair, and went silently downstairs to her solitary room.

*   *   *

Two years after the death of her husband, Verena remarried, to provide a father for her three children. Walter and Anna had long since married and, in the spring, Heini and Dorli had likewise started families. At the beginning of summer, Ruedi also left the parental home to take up a position as steward in Hermetswil.

Only the fourteen year old Emma and Nicholas, two years junior, remained with the mother. Thus, little by little, a hush had descended upon the large farmhouse, which would soon become quieter still. It was young Nicholas. He fared like the swallows in autumn: a kind of innate restlessness drove him irresistibly into the distance.

He was, in many ways, the image of Klaus and so claimed the mother's full affection. What distinguished him from the father, however, was his sensitive, fickle nature, his delicate health and dreamy disposition.

He liked most of all to sit by the hearth with his mother and listen to her stories. Or he climbed fir trees or rocks and from there looked out into the valley for hours, until Emma called him for a meal. Once, late in the evening, she found him contemplating on a great boulder above the Melchaa. "Look!" said the precocious lad pointing to the white spray, "everything passes away, everything!"

Of all the legends, he preferred the one about the unfortunate countess Genevieve von Brabant. The history of the holy beggar Alexius, he knew by heart. His craving for such stories was insatiable. He had therefore also learnt to read exceptionally early, taught by his mother in the course of lonely winter evenings. The parish priest of Kerns taught him to write and when he made his way home from his evening lesson, he regularly stopped at Ranft where the father had him scribble his new letters on the slate! Ultimately, the new Ranft chaplain drummed a bit of Latin into him.

One day, while tidying up the attic, Dorothy had found a yellowed breviary. It probably belonged to Klaus' great-uncle, a priest who in his later years had said the early Mass in Stans. Admittedly, rats had nibbled at the first pages of the neat little vellum books and the dampness had left reddish-brown stains. Yet in spite of that, her son's eyes sparkled when at Easter she presented him with the spruced-up volumes. For hours he would shut himself away in the children's room, where - amidst his strange collection of twisted roots, glittering crystals and pressed alpine flowers - he recited the breviary. In his bedroom he had also made a little wooden altar, upon which, in the company of Walter's eldest boy, he chanted the High Mass. Although he went about these things unaffectedly and was himself not aware of it for a long time, a yearning for the Priesthood of Jesus Christ gradually stirred and blossomed within him.

Dorothy was crushed when, on a pilgrimage to Our Lady of Schwändi, he finally revealed this to her. She knew too well that this divine call meant an impending separation for long years to come, perhaps even forever. And Nicholas was her last son, as well as the last living memento of her husband.

The day for goodbyes arrived at a gallop. The old wound in Dorothy's heart which she had suffered at each other farewell, was again torn open... Nicholas was unaware of just how much he reminded her of his father, to what extent he renewed his father's "adieu."

It was the beginning of October, Feast of the Holy Guardian Angels. Autumn had arrived early. Red and yellow foliage littered the fields and in the morning the first white frost shimmered atop the grey roofing. The previous day, Nicholas had been to receive his father's blessing. He returned home melancholy and reticent. Together with his mother, who was red-eyed but resigned, he packed his small knapsack: Dorothy included some linen, a pot of honey and a relic of St. Nicholas von Myre that Klaus had given her shortly before their wedding, and he squeezed in his few books between the socks and shirts.

The following morning before cock-crow, Dorothy took a candle and went into the children's room to wake Nicholas with one last kiss. She found him already awake, however, and abandoned her plan... The boy jumped out of bed and threw on his clothes without even looking at his mother.

In the meantime, Walter had arrived. He had offered to accompany his baby brother - his "Benjamin," as he fondly called him - to Basel, where the university was located. Emma was also present. She brushed the dust from her brother's smock and wept - her last playmate, now abandoning the fold.

When the final moment had come, the mother traced a small cross on the forehead of her youngest child.

"May God guide you, my Nicholas!" she said softly. She did not cry; but her lips were quivering and she could not utter another word. Still one last time she caressed his frizzy hair, then escorted her two sons to the garden gate.

"Take care of the child, Walter!" she cried out to the elder as her eyes followed the two disparate figures disappearing behind the fruit trees. When their footsteps were drowned in the rumbling of the Melchaa she again turned back to the house.

Around evening, Dorothy became feverish. Emma had to put her to bed. It had all been too much! Once more she had had to bear the harsh sacrifice of St. Gallus' Day, 1467. Again and again she saw her husband in her son, and her lifeblood poured out afresh from that scar she thought had healed long ago.

Emma spent the night at her mother's bedside: she dreamed and spoke incoherently. Approaching midnight, just as the young girl was dozing off, the patient abruptly sat upright, extended her arms towards the door and cried: "Klaus, Klaus, don't leave! Please stay!... stay..."

Finally, at 4 a.m., as the bell down in The Ranft rang for Mass, she fell into a deep sleep.

*   *   *

Two years after her brother's departure, Dorli had a son whom she baptised Konrad. He was already Dorothy's fourteenth grandchild, yet with her fifty years and fresh complexion she was quite a young grandmother.

Her hair, however, gradually became pale and thin and her face was increasingly laced with a web of fine wrinkles... Not long after the baptism of Konrad, her health began to wane. It was not a specific ailment; a little nausea in the morning, listlessness during the day and some passing dizzy spells if she over-exerted herself.

The winter had been dry, but severely cold nonetheless. Dorothy caught a chill while breaking up the ice in the fount and despite a valiant struggle, a dreadful fever eventually flattened her in early December. For two or three days she hovered between life and death. They called the children who lived outside the district. They also gave Klaus a daily report on the course of the illness but, true to his intention, he did not come.

The Saturday after the Feast of St. Thomas, Peter, who had built himself a small house eighteen months after his brother's departure, came visiting in the evening.

"Bad news!" he said on entering, without regard for the condition of the sick who lay pale and hollow-cheeked in her cushions.

"Welcome Peter!" she said with a tired smile, motioning to the stool at the foot of her bed.

He overlooked the invitation and remained standing.

"And so, what is it that's so bad?" she asked quietly.

Without further ado, Peter sat on the table and opened up: "You know that the Diet is currently meeting in Stans?" She nodded. "Well! Yet *again* it's a fine mess! The cities want to lumber us with two new city members, Freiburg and Solothurn.

In that case we, in the country, we'll have no more say at all with all these cities. It's the last straw! Who created it, the Confederation? Us or the great gentlemen of Berne and Zurich? Besides, Zurich... what a disaster! Ever since it was accepted into the Confederacy its arrogant stubborness has caused nothing but strife. The refined Bernese are perhaps a little more flexible than them; but you can see in the way they treat people from Obwald that they don't rate farmers very highly... We don't want to have to grovel before these merchants!"

"Take it easy, Peter!" soothed Dorothy. "They have their faults it's true, just like us; but have they not also, like us, sworn perpetual alliance?"

Peter, however, paid no attention to the calming words - he was on fire!

"Now they want to admit this Solothurn, of all places, that has the same red and white Standard as us - I saw it clearly three weeks ago when they visited Klaus! And then these half-Latin Freiburgers: French rabble, loudmouths and lazy!"

"Peter!" she objected softly. "Did they not fight alongside our men at Murten?"

"Yes, of course! But only to save their own hides. They would've been among the first to have had their city raised to the ground by The Bold! What's more," he thundered, thumping the table, "we don't *need* the cities! We fought for and won freedom without them and we'll keep it without them!"

After he caught his breath, he went quiet for a while before adding, eyes lowered: "I do not understand, truly, why Klaus is always flirting with these cities. Because it's clear that he supports them; you only have to see all their messengers coming and going from his place."

He had not yet finished speaking when Hans appeared.

"Things are not good down in Stans," he said upon entering. He offered his hand to his mother, who held it fast, looking up at her burly son.

"They cannot agree?" she asked.

"I was down there representing our Council," he began, "and have seen and heard everything with my own eyes and ears. The situation now, is that the two cities want to be admitted as full and equal members of the Confederation and the country constituents won't accept them as such. The Solothurner yelled 'All or nothing!' at which our chief official called out across the room: 'Who precisely are the applicants here? You or us?' It can't go on like that! We'll have war within two or three days, barring a miracle!"

"Don't you know Hans, that Father is praying just for that?" said the mother.

"Klaus? What can he do about it?" grumbled Peter.

"Of course, he's had a hand in affairs for months," admitted Hans grudgingly, "but now it would take power and money - and he has nothing!"

"Sacrifice carries more weight than power and wealth," said Dorothy gently.

"Forget these Lords of the city," Peter went on. "Let them keep their cosy city alliance - their *Burgrecht* agreement - and let's keep our Confederation! What do these arrogant men matter to us?"

"No, Uncle!" interjected Hans resolutely. "Things are not so simple. They saw during the Zurich war that the rural cantons would have starved without the cities. And without Berne, we would've had Charles the Bold and his Burgundians right on our borders! But *they* also need *us*. We simply belong together! And if we break apart now, then no power on earth will be able to put the pieces together again - ever!"

He stopped and looked at the flickering night-light. There was a lull... just the gurgling of the fount under its thick icy shell, the purring of the cat, curled up on the warm fleece at Dorothy's feet, and then, gradually, the crunching of snow as the light footsteps of a child drew near.

The door was pushed slightly open - just enough to let through the freckled head of a young boy. "Grandmother, may I come in?" he asked. "Naturally, my child!" called the grandmother, and a smile flitted across her dull features.

He entered. It was Hans' thirteen year old son, his eldest and the grandmother's favourite. There were many reasons why: apart from being her first grandchild, he had been born within a month of Klaus' departure. Moreover, his name was also Nicholas.

"Father! Mother says to tell you that a Council messenger has come and has said that everything is alright in Stans!" he recited faithfully to his father.

"That *cannot* be right!" exclaimed Peter in disbelief. "It's a canard!"

The grandmother seized the little angel of peace and hugged him. Hans was ready to rush out when Walter burst in, excited and breathless.

"Mother!" he cried, barely halfway through the door. "Father has saved the country!"

Dorothy was beaming; Peter shook his head. Hans asked coolly: "How did this change come about?"

"Well, here it is: yesterday evening, all they did was squabble amongst themselves; this morning, they came within a hairs-breadth of drawing swords.

"But that night, Father am Grund from Stans set out for Ranft. He spoke with Father for an hour or two and hurried back again, as fast as he could. When he arrived, he managed to get the deputies - who had already packed their bags! - to meet together once again. What he said to them, nobody knows for sure - but after a two hour meeting, *everything* was sorted out, the new Covenant sealed and Freiburg and Solothurn admitted."

He had delivered his report enthusiastically, speaking more to the two men. Now he turned to the woman.

"You see, Mother! It's him, it's our Father's work. Everyone is saying it!"

The first jubilant smile for many years heightened Dorothy's already radiant expression. "The miracle has happened, Hans!" she said, casting a pointed glance at her eldest.

At that moment a bell began to toll in the valley, then two, three, four, and a whole chorus. The bell of St. Niklausen also joined in and the mountains resounded with their solemn rejoicing... Then, for an instant, amidst the weighty tones of the great ringing, there rose the pure, innocent sound of a little bell - it was The Ranft chapel!

Dorothy wept.

"It was not in vain," she stammered tearfully.

"No, Mother," Walter confirmed, "you see: it was not in vain!"

*   *   *

Five years had passed since the event of Stans. In the house on the Flüe pasture, life went on its slow, modest way. At The Ranft, on the other hand, hardly a day passed without a visitor calling: messengers-of-state in coloured robes, couriers with batons in the colours of their canton, distinguished ambassadors from abroad, theologians and abbots. In addition, and just as disturbing, came the sick, those wanting advice and riff-raff of all kinds.

Dorothy withdrew into the background more and more and her visits to Ranft became even less frequent. Besides, Klaus called her ever more rarely and she had made a principle of going only if he invited her.

When she saw him again on Christmas Eve, it struck her how he had aged. His skin felt like leather to the touch and his face was grey, as if covered in dust.

At the beginning of March, she was informed that Brother Klaus had caught a heavy cold. Two days later, it was said that he had a fever. She had to stop herself from running down to him immediately. Obedience alone restrained her.

On the Feast of St. Benedict, the sexton arrived and said that Brother Klaus wanted her to come as he was nearing his end. Dorothy threw a woollen shawl over herself, called Emma, sent the stable-boy to look for Hans and Walter and ran, as fast as her weak legs could carry her, down into The Ranft.

Wafts of murky-grey mist crawled through the woods and the last snow lay here and there like leaves on the yellow grass.

When both women stepped into the cell, they hit a wall of foul-smelling air. In the gloomy candlelight, Dorothy recognised old Erny Anderhalden, who leant motionless against the wall. She also made out the Ranft chaplain, standing in the corner in surplice and stole.

"He has just received Holy Viaticum," the priest whispered to the new arrivals. "Now he's lost consciousness."

Dorothy heard a groan and suddenly realised that the dying was stretched out on the floor, his head turned towards the chapel. She knelt down beside him and began to caress the bony hand, which insistently pushed away a threadbare blanket.

The supple, feminine touch revived him a little. His eyes wandered around a while in the dark, then fastened on the woman, whose features he studied attentively for some time. Eventually he recognised her, began moving his lips and at last whispered, arduously: "Oh, Dorli! How happy I am that we're together in Heaven!"

"We're not yet quite so far...," she replied with the trace of a smile.

"We'll soon be there, both and forever!"

He closed his eyes, as if to gather himself. After a while he looked at her again and said: "I've caused you more pain than all our children together, poor Dorli... For your "yes," *I* don't thank you - God will thank you!"

An involuntary shiver passed through the emaciated figure.

As Dorothy wiped the sweat from his temples he seized her hand and said: "Soon, we'll be united forever!"

She pressed his fingertips to her lips and sobbed: "Yes, yes!"

A long silence followed. Only the groan of the wind and the wheezing breath of the dying man filled the cell. Then the door below grated and the stairs creaked. Hans and Walter appeared in the doorway. They nodded a bashful greeting. Walter went down on one knee near his father, while Hans, arms folded, remained standing in the shadowy light. Klaus no longer recognised them.

All of a sudden he raised himself up on his elbow and stared blankly at the little window, which framed the soft red glow of the sanctuary lamp. "I'm coming... I'm coming, Lord!" he gasped, as if answering a call from the altar. After a pause, still turned towards the ruby light, he smiled and whispered gently: "Yes, Dorothy too... "

The chaplain bent down to him, seeking an explanation of the last words: "Dorothy too, will receive the eternal crown with you - is that true?"

Klaus did not answer; he merely repeated: "My Lord and my God - My Lord and my all!"

A liberating quiver suddenly flashed across the exhausted body - she alone saw it... The death rattle faded... the eyes closed.

The priest raised his voice and prayed aloud: *"In paradisum deducant te angeli...* May the holy angels lead you into paradise... and with Lazarus, who was once a poor man, may you enjoy eternal rest!"

"Amen," answered Dorothy firmly.

*   *   *

Three days later, from early morning on, streams of people flocked to The Ranft. The little chapel could accommodate very few and the great majority of them trudged around in the snow and waited.

A whisper ran through the crowd when a woman veiled in black, with a young man on either arm, came down the path. It was Dorothy.

She paid no heed to the hundred priests in surplice standing outside the chapel, nor to the line of state officials that stretched as far as the bier. She had eyes only for the dead man laid out before the altar and stitched up in a coarse sack. She stopped at the bier, bowed to the corpse and remained standing there for a while, perfectly still, her face obscured by a heavy black scarf. On a signal from *Landamann* Hans von Flüe, Chief Magistrate of Obwalden, eight dignitaries stepped forward and lifted the meagre load onto their shoulders. The cortege set off...

Dorothy, who walked arm in arm with Hans, felt as if finally awaking from a long, bad dream. For decades she had watched her husband skirting the dark and mortal depths, unable to help. How many times had she not wanted to fly down to Ranft to sustain him in his struggle, to at least mop his brow; but even the humble joy of service had been denied her. Now, he had been snatched from her forever. Yet she knew too that he was at last safely home. Today, One far greater was mopping his sweaty brow. Of that, she was certain!

Everything was better again! Her broken heart and the terrible solitude; the bloody rushes of indignation and the bottomless wellspring of her tears - all healed, vanquished, dried up. Yet how was it possible - in this eerie mist, with the leaden weight of her limbs... how could she feel so light-hearted?

It was only below in Sachseln, as they slowly lowered the body into the tomb, that she fully understood and it radiated joyfully through her whole being: "Klaus is not there in the cold stone. Klaus is again walking beside you - and so forever!"

*   *   *

The day after the funeral was a bleak, damp winter's day. The snow was wet and heavy and even the lake appeared muddy.

Dorothy had been to the grave and was walking back up to the house, puffing. After all the sleepless nights, and the shock, her mind was blank. Even her heartache was numb.

As she was passing over a small bridge, she heard some urgent, youthful steps behind her. Automatically, she turned around. There standing next to her was a handsome, sun tanned youth. He greeted her with exquisite courtesy and informed her that he had seen, up there on the steep rock-face, surrounded by heavenly light and holding in his hand a flag featuring a bear's claw, the deceased Nicholas.

Dorothy looked up at the rocky escarpment but saw nothing more than dark, desolate trees and some patches of snow between them. Her eyes searched the surrounding area, then she looked back to the youth - but he had vanished. She shook her head and resumed her steep path home... What exactly did the bears claw signify? The thing did not seem completely novel to her and she mused and brooded, combing her memory.

Finally, when she had arrived up at Flüeli, she recalled a vision that Klaus had related to her many years before. A nobleman had appeared to him and said: "Nicholas, if you stand firm to the end, the bear's claw - the banner of victory - will be yours." So Klaus had triumphed; he now dwelt in the Divine Light!

"Lord God," Dorothy prayed, "Thou art good, and all that Thou doest is good!"

*   *   *

Barely a day passed without Dorothy wending her way down to Sachseln.

On a beautiful May morning, when everything around her was humming and fragrant and even children along the way called out to her more gaily than usual, "Good morning, Frau Dorothy!" - she arrived wearier than ever at the graveyard.

While walking around the church tower, she had to lean against the wall several times because her feet refused to carry her any further. Thus she reached the portico, where Klaus lay buried under a weighty stone slab. After sprinkling some drops of holy water over the grave, she took refuge in the most remote corner. It was her favourite spot; for there she could linger silently, undisturbed and unseen.

Dorothy had lost track of time, sitting there, when she heard the piercing scream of a child from the street. Some moments later, a family of three - father, mother and daughter - entered into the half-light of the consecrated space. The father, young and strong, carried the girl of about ten years who was writhing in his arms like a miserable little mite. She was deathly pale and the mother, walking beside her, was constantly wiping yellowish foam from her mouth.

Without noticing the old woman in the corner, the three headed towards the tomb. The mother sank to her knees and kissed the stone where the name of the deceased was engraved. The man stood there squarely, holding the sick child firmly under the arms.

All at once the girl began to lash out, all her limbs tensed as if to breaking point and a vile slime gushed from her cruelly twisted mouth. The father was clearly unprepared for the attack because he let go of the child, who fell thrashing about onto the slab. Dorothy stifled a fearful cry!

Father and mother cautiously picked up the child. She was not injured. Better still, the convulsions had passed... Fresh colour slowly filled the sunken cheeks... and - miracle! - the child was smiling!

The man stood there rooted to the spot; his wife covered the girl with loving kisses.

Eventually, the father composed himself and fell to his knees. The woman and the girl did likewise and thus they remained a long time - so long, that Dorothy thought they would never leave.

At last, the man murmured in a quavering, tear-choked voice: "Our dear Brother Klaus! You've given us back our little Dorli - we thank you!"

As they left, the eyes of the little girl and the old woman met. Dorothy's skin crawled: never before had she seen pure light stream from the eyes of a human being!

"Yes, Klaus. It was not in vain!" she whispered, then knelt down before his grave and prayed:

"Almighty God, Thine is the wisdom, Thine is the power. Thou alone knowest why Thou dost give and why Thou dost take; why Thou dost unite us and why Thou dost separate us. May Thy name be praised forever. Amen. Alleluia!"

*   *   *

The young Klaus, after studying in Paris, went on to become a Doctor of Theology and later parish priest of Sachseln, where Dorothy spent some time with him at the presbytery. He died in 1503, only 16 years after his father.

With this early death of her beloved son, Dorothy steadily withdrew into solitude. She welcomed it, since it allowed her to live undisturbed with her memories. And while her mind was nearly always at the cemetery, her body became frail, the soft, round face angular and the bright eyes misty.

Ensconced for hours before her dowry chest, she drew out the gold coin that Klaus had once received as a soldier, rubbed it with her apron and let it gleam in the sunlight. She passed her fingers carefully over the sharp edge of a dagger or caressed with loving hands the coarse penitential cord that the Ranft chaplain had removed from the dead man and entrusted to her.

Not infrequently, she threw a woollen scarf across her trembling shoulders and cautiously descended the steep slope to his hermitage. Admittedly, the cell had been sealed and awaited, perhaps, a new occupant. But she walked around the little house, stroking the knotty beams, running her fingertips across the fine moss lodged in the cracks, and watching reverently the zealous hustle and bustle of the beetles as they crawled up and down, to and fro...

When she had finally seen enough, she went to the chapel and gently opened the door, careful not to disturb the solemnity of a silence broken only by the rushing organ of the Melchaa and the hum of the bees. She sat down in the last pew, and prayed and dreamed... dreamed and prayed...

One evening - when the whole countryside seemed numb and the arid Melchaa was no more than a murmur - the Ranft chaplain came to close the side door. An old woman, however, was still there in the very last pew, under the small window. In the darkness, he could not recognise her and from the entrance he called out: "Hey there, good woman, it's time! I have to close!"

The old woman sat there.

The priest went down and, a little rudely, nudged her. She still did not stir, but her head veered slowly onto her left shoulder.

The man caught his breath and shone the lantern into her face.

The mouth was smiling; but the eyes slept.

She was dead.

The startled priest rushed out to fetch help, leaving the door wide-open. A cool mountain breeze swirled in. The sanctuary lamp reddened. A bittersweet scent of resin and sifted hay engulfed the altar... and filled the House of God.

The seventeenth century baroque parish church in Sachseln containing the remains and relics of Brother Klaus.

Pope John Paul II prays before Brother Klaus' sarcophagus in the parish church (June 14, 1984).

At the canonisation ceremony on 15 May, 1947, clergy from the canton of Obwalden lead an image of the new Saint, in which he carries his standard - a white flag imprinted with a bear's claw, signalling heavenly victory through his perseverance to the end.

Two miraculously healed through the intercession of Brother Klaus. On 26 June, 1937, upon being blessed with a relic of the Saint in the Sachseln parish church, the then 27- year-old Ida Jecker, right, was instantly and completely healed of her epilepsy, the total paralysis of her left arm, a related suppurating ulcer and unbearably painful open wounds - all of which she had suffered for many years. Left, Anna Melchior who was cured on the day of canonisation (see Preface).

REFLECTION

Should Nicholas von Flüe have left his wife and children? This is the question that threatens to obscure the grandeur of the destiny related in this book. In weighing our response, we should bear in mind the following facts:

Firstly: each true marital union is indissoluble. On that subject, the laws of Nature and the still clearer precepts of Divine Revelation permit no doubt.

Secondly: in either case - i.e. both in Nature and Revelation - it is God Who, through His demands, manifests His absolute sovereignty.

Thirdly: God, being our Supreme Master, has the right even to dispose of the bonds of marriage. Moreover, we already acknowledge this unconsciously when death, as messenger of the Divine Will, severs the marriage bonds.

Fourthly: for the believer, therefore, the possibility of breaking the conjugal life of a couple, even while both are alive, falls perfectly within the prerogatives of divine power. In so doing, however, God never infringes upon that royal gift of our Free Will. He calls, He suggests; but man - in this case, husband and wife - freely decides.

Fifthly: the demand to leave his family is and will always be an exceptional case and God only has recourse to it with a view to accomplishing a higher good.

Has God really called me? That was the crucial question Klaus never ceased to ask himself. It was his cross and his bitter beatitude. God's response was the miracle of total fast, the day at

Stans and the solace and peace which radiated in such wonderful ways from the hermit of Ranft. These are all infallible marks of a special, divine election, before whose mysterious, unfathomable depths our initial, all too human question is reduced to silence.

God is able to dissolve that which He has joined - most certainly! Yet He does not do it without the consent of the two beings bound together in love for eternity. In Klaus, this "yes" matured slowly and painfully. With Dorothy, it burst forth suddenly and tempestuously from her heart. "Only your free consent can release me to live alone with God," Klaus told her. Thus, he left in her hands his vocation, his holiness and - as they only came to realise later - the salvation of the beloved Fatherland.

This story was about that "Yes" - its first irruption, blind and cruel; its gradual maturation; its final transfiguration. That Klaus followed God's call, is his holiness and greatness. That Dorothy gave that call her "Yes", is her imperishable crown.

ST. NICHOLAS VON FLÜE

A Short History

The kingdom of God is not a matter of eating and drinking this or that; it means rightness of heart, finding our peace and our joy in the Holy Spirit. Such is the badge of Christ's service which wins acceptance with God, and the good opinion of our fellow men. Let our aim, then, be peace, and strengthening one another's faith.

Romans 14, 17-19

St. Nicholas von Flüe, canonised in 1947 and known by the Swiss simply as Brother Klaus, was born at a time when neither Europe nor Switzerland existed as the entities we know today. The late Middle Ages in which he lived and worked out his salvation - in the most diverse roles of farmer, soldier, father of ten children, politician, magistrate, statesman, hermit and mystic - was a time of great turbulence. Ongoing battles, both physical and spiritual, racked communities everywhere. Grasping, short-sighted secular leaders waged meaningless and bloody wars while dissension and scandal tore at the Mystical Body of Christ, The Holy Catholic Church, through one or other of the seven deadly sins which held sway in many ecclesiastical quarters.

The idea of the nation-state was still developing and that unrivalled symbol of an emerging sense of nationality, St. Joan of Arc, was executed aged 19 when Nicholas was only 14 years old. Five years after his death, Christopher Columbus discovered a continent and the idea of Europe acquired a new dimension.

Certain technological advances were also taking place and with the invention of the printing press, for example, books began to multiply; the first book about Brother Klaus appearing in Nuremberg, probably in 1487, the year of his death.

Within this historic, volatile and troubled milieu, which mirrors that of our own era in so many ways, Nicholas faced the problems of daily life with candour and originality. As Father Cyril, O.A.R., has written:

"Though a hermit and a mystic, Nicholas did not run away from the burning issues of his contemporaries. On the contrary, he single-mindedly steered the destiny of his country towards new directions, prevailing over exaggerated and conflicting patriotisms and tribalisms of his fellow citizens by emphasising confederation and peaceful neutrality. He is an attractive individual who recoiled from political imperialism as well as from religious triumphalism and the quest for power. "

EARLY LIFE

In the heart of Switzerland, within the area between Lucerne and Interlaken, lies the small canton of Unterwalden which in turn is divided into two "half-cantons": Nidwalden with its capital at Stans, and Obwalden whose capital is Sarnen. In a mountainous region of Obwalden above the village of Sachseln on Lake Sarnen, is the hamlet of Flüeli (formerly Flüe) where Brother Klaus was born on 21 March 1417. Ten minutes east of Flüeli, in a deep gorge through which flows a mountain torrent called the Melchaa, lie a few acres of grassy slopes and woodland known as The Ranft. In this tranquil place is a tiny wooden hermitage, attached to a small chapel, where Nicholas died exactly seventy years later.

This central region of Switzerland is the nucleus from which the modern Confederation developed. In the late 13th century, representatives of what are now the cantons of Unterwalden, Uri and Schwyz (which later gave its name to the whole country) met in a meadow overlooking Lake Lucerne and swore perpetual alliance against their common foes. This event is still celebrated annually on 1 August with bonfires and fireworks.

Progressively during the 14th century the original three grew to eight. In the following century their fortunes became entangled with their powerful and militant neighbours: The Kings of France and the Dukes of Burgundy to the west, the Habsburgs to the north and east and the Dukes of Milan and Savoy to the south. The shifting alliances of these powers with each other and with the Confederates form the background to Brother Klaus' life.

The young Confederation was at its peak when Nicholas was born. The Austrians, the last bitter opponents of their independence, had been defeated in a glorious victory at The Battle of Sempach and further alliances and conquests had consolidated their liberty. Young and old were full of patriotic ardour and vigorously involved in the political affairs of the country. Klaus' forebears had been identified with the struggle for independence and his parents, Heini and Emma, were farmers and leaders in the local community. In 15th century Unterwalden, boys acquired the right to vote at the age of fourteen and so by 1431 Klaus was already attending meetings of the *Landsgemeinde* (local council) with his father.

From the earliest days of his youth, despite the punishing physical regimen associated with farm work in a harsh climate, Nicholas found time for extra prayer and fasting. Erny Rohrer, his intimate friend since childhood days, later testified to his piety: "He began this [fasting] when he was still quite a young boy and for a long time fasted every Friday, later four days a week, as well as the whole [Lenten] fast when he would eat nothing all day but a small piece of bread or a few dried pears. But he did this secretly, so as not to show off. And if he was asked about it, or reproached by some who thought he would not be able to bare it, he always said: 'God will have it so.' "

The dissensions and generally deplorable situation in the Catholic Church at that time, which led to a lack of readily available spiritual direction - just as today - must have weighed heavily on Nicholas throughout his adolescence. For political reasons, there was no resident priest in his own parish and the presbytery remained empty for a further ten years after his birth. Nicholas was therefore baptised in nearby Kerns. When priests finally arrived in Sachseln, tension and disputes between the priests and parishioners became a sad feature of parish life that was to continue throughout his lifetime.

Yet Klaus never lost faith in the Church, nor did he abandon his parish - even while leading lawsuits against the unjust demands and behaviour of Church and clergy. Instead, he was prepared to travel long distances to seek the orthodox spiritual nourishment and inspiration he so ardently desired. His mother, Emma Ruobert, came from the village of Wolfenschiessen near Engelberg where a much revered hermit, Matthias Hattinger, was associated with a lay movement called the Friends of God. Like Nicholas, its members sought union with the Supreme Good by entering into themselves through prayer and austerity. We can reasonably presume that he personally visited Brother Hattinger and it is believed that many of Klaus' friends and advisers belonged to this deeply spiritual movement, including Father Heini am Grund, who played an important part in his life. When Klaus left home in 1467, it is thought that his original intention was to join a community of the Friends of God in Strasbourg.

From the age of sixteen, Klaus became liable for military service. During his lifetime there were twenty-eight wars and military campaigns and he took part in several of them, rising to the rank of Captain. For ten years from 1436 there was civil war between Zurich on the one side, which had entered into an alliance with the despised Austrians, and the remaining

Confederates on the other.

As the noble, disinterested goals of their ancestors gradually gave way to a desire for conquest and wealth, however, Nicholas was increasingly troubled by the warlike spirit and loose morals that the frequent campaigns and notorious slaughters engendered in his compatriots. For a man who took seriously the much neglected teachings and principles of his Catholic faith - that only love, mutual respect and justice for all could ensure peaceful co-existence - Klaus must have been shocked by the failure to observe the rules of warfare laid down by the Covenant of Sempach, signed by the Confederates in 1393, and by the breaking of solemn agreements. Nonetheless, when the tocsin called him to take up arms he obeyed because he was convinced that submission to authority constituted the fundamental principle of civil life, just as he knew that true soldierly virtue consisted in being obedient as well as courageous.

Both Erny Rohrer and another lifelong friend, Erny Anderhalden, testified after Klaus' death that "even in war he did his enemies little injury, but drew aside and prayed and protected them as far as lay in his power." This conduct and attitude is confirmed in all scholarly research on Nicholas from the earliest biographies. His regular experience of the brutality of war also saw him become a vigorous opponent of the so-called "pension-system," whereby regular payments were made to leading persons in the cantons in return for providing troops to fight in foreign armies. It was a constantly recurring political, social and economic problem during his lifetime. In addition to the official levies, individuals enlisted independently as mercenaries (this is the origin of the term "free-lance"). During the fifteenth century the Swiss had gained a reputation as the most efficient soldiers in Europe, even when outnumbered and defeated, and their services were much sought after. But political and social complications were great. When they returned from foreign service, having lost the habit of regular work, the soldiers were lawless and predatory. The problem occupied the Diet intermittently for decades. Three hundred years later, it was a contingent of Swiss Guards that defended Louis XVI when the Tuileries was stormed. Brother Klaus' advice to abandon the system, though often quoted in contemporary chronicles, was disregarded. After his death, his two sons, Hans and Walter are both recorded as accepting payments for supplying troops when holding the office of *Landamman*. The system was not finally abolished until 1859 - an exception being made for the Papal Guard.

FAMILY LIFE

In his late twenties, Nicholas married a farmer's daughter, Dorothea Wyss, from Mount Schwändi on the other side of Lake Sarnen. She was probably not more than sixteen, possibly even younger, at the time of their marriage around 1445. He took her to live in a house he built himself a few hundred yards from his parents' home. In the course of the next two decades, ten children were born: five boys and five girls. Periods of absence from home while on military service continued for some years after his marriage and Hans, their first child, was born in 1447; Nicholas, the youngest, 20 years later.

He worked extremely hard on the land, as Hans later testified, and became a prosperous farmer with a title-free property and a main estate that yielded enough fodder to feed thirty head of cattle. Alongside this ordinary routine of work on the farm, instructing his children and hearing Mass on Sundays, Klaus served as a councillor and magistrate and represented his community when required.

Due to missing records, the exact details of Klaus' periods of office are not known, but he probably succeeded his father and once, in 1462, he represented Obwalden at a meeting of the four "Forest Cantons" (the three original cantons plus Lucerne) in a dispute with the Church. In another lawsuit, Klaus and his friend Erny Rohrer took a leading part in resisting the unjust demands of the absentee priest for a tithe of the local fruit harvest, though giving no service in return. They won the case.

In surviving records, he often heads the list of deputations appointed by the village or commune to deal with some local dispute. In line with the Swiss practice of rotating the more important offices - for instance to this day the presidency of the Swiss Confederation - Klaus would have succeeded to the office of *Landamman* (sheriff or chief magistrate) in due course had he not, according to all accounts, "resisted strenuously." He became increasingly disturbed by the dishonesty and corruption he encountered even among his fellow magistrates and finally he resigned. He told his family that he had seen fire issuing from the mouths of his fellow justices. Another record says that the final break came because he was unable to prevent an unjust judgement reached by bribery and other pressures. Perhaps this is why the relevant list of office-holders has disappeared.

Alongside his very active family and civic life, an insistent call to further deepen his spiritual life was growing within Klaus. As an increasingly afluent society abandoned the frugality and simplicity of earlier times, lapsing into covetousness, envy and greed, he lived more and more in the realm of those supernatural values *"which no thief comes near, no moth consumes."* He told his friend Erny Anderhalden many years later, that at the age of sixteen he had had a vision of a beautiful tower rising up in The Ranft gorge where the chapel and his hermitage now stand. It was because of this vision that he had always been inclined to seek solitude. Hans relates how his father would go to bed at the same time as the rest of the family but at night get up and go down to The Ranft.

There is more than one account of how, when he and Hans were clearing brambles in the upper Melchtal valley, Klaus was attacked by Satan and was hurled over a boundary ridge (a drop between two levels on a steep alp) and lay unconscious till his son picked him up. Hans reported that when his father finally came to, still feeling very shaken, all he said was: "Well in God's name that was a bad turn the Devil did me, but I suppose it was all according to God's will."

If Klaus was aware from an early age that God had some special task for him - he even told his advisor Father am Grund a strange tale of pre-natal memories foreshadowing his destiny - it was a different matter to know the precise nature of that *something*. In the meantime, as Providence would have it, he was gaining much wisdom through his ordinary duties as family man and citizen which he no doubt called upon later in life to advise the crowds of people who sought his help.

The spirit in which he lived out his inner conflict to discern the Will of God during this time, is captured in a haunting petition which has come to be known as *Brother Klaus' Prayer:*

> O Lord, take Thou from me
> All that makes me turn from Thee.
>
> O Lord, give Thou to me
> All that draws me nearer Thee.
>
> O Lord, take myself from me.
> Give me all and whole to Thee.

THE BREAK

In his mid-forties, as the tension between God's call and his worldly ties became more and more unbearable, Klaus suffered a severe depression. Some years later he told a visiting friar that for two years "he could find no peace by day or night but was brought so low that even my dear wife and the company of my children were a burden to me." While he was in this state, his "intimate and trusted friend" Heini am Grund, then parish priest of Kriens, came to see him. The priest suggested all sorts of remedies, none of which were effective. He then explained to Klaus how to divide his meditation on the Passion between the seven canonical hours. Klaus welcomed this suggestion and put it into practice at once, but "because I was involved in many worldly affairs and official responsibilities I found... my meditation lacked concentration." So he began to withdraw more and more to The Ranft. Perhaps woodcuts illustrating the Passion helped Klaus, who could neither read nor write, to memorise the subject of each meditation.

This exercise, directing his thoughts away from himself at regular intervals throughout the day, steadied him and allowed him to clarify his path. One learned commentator suggested that at some time during this period he must have consulted Heini am Grund about the insistent call to leave home, and received the advice that it could hardly be a call from God if he could not obtain his wife's agreement.

Understandably, obtaining Dorothy's consent was not easy. The love and fidelity Nicholas had afforded her throughout their married life had made her very happy and the decision was probably harder for her than for Nicholas. The bedroom they shared for twenty years can still be seen in their wonderfully preserved house in Flüeli, as also the stove in the living-room where he knelt to pray in the night and the door he left unlatched when he strode through the darkness to The Ranft. Yet Dorothy was a profoundly Catholic woman who placed the fulfilment of God's Will above all else. She only desired that the actions and aspirations of her husband and children conform to that Divine Will.

There is no contemporary record of the discussions they had, but the earliest official biographer, the Bernese humanist Heini Wölflin (1501), claims to have used accounts from reliable witnesses:

"He unfolded his plan to his beloved wife, who was also his trusted advisor: he had resolved to put the attractions of the world behind him and to seek out a suitable place where in solitude he could devote himself entirely to spiritual contemplation. He took great pains to persuade her, since her agreement was necessary, but for a long time his efforts were in vain, because of all the domestic complications. On his side he remained convinced that his whole way of life at present was incompatible with his vow to renounce the world, so he continued to urge her in spite of her entreaties, and at last reluctantly she gave her consent."

From a distance of 500 years, it is perhaps difficult for some to understand the attraction of a hermit's life of prayer and solitude, devoid of human companionship and creature comforts. In the Middle Ages, however, it was a most natural thing and the presence of hermits was considered a great blessing and heavenly consolation - in the same way that *faithful* priests and religious are still regarded by Catholic's today. Nonetheless, it was just as extraordinary then as it would be now for a man to turn away from his honoured civic duties, his possessions *and* growing family to embrace this life of poverty, extreme fasting and total immersion in the things of God. Yet that is precisely what Klaus did on 16 October, 1467, St. Gallus' Day - St. Gallus was the Irish monk who had left home 800 years earlier to preach the gospel in Switzerland - when he set off at dawn barefoot and bareheaded, in a coarse brown robe with a girdle of rope and carrying no more than a staff and a rosary. We can hardly imagine the pain Dorothy must have felt and yet, according to tradition, she wove his cope herself. As Father Cyril writes: "We stand here before a spiritual event that, from a distance of five centuries, we can observe but with a sense of deep awe. Here we stand on numinous ground, sensing the unfathomable depths of a soul touched by God."

On his way to join the Friends of God in Strasbourg, he soon reached Liestal, between Lucerne and Basel, but saw the village as if completely engulfed by red flames. He thus sought shelter in a nearby farmhouse. The farmer, apparently unable to see any lurid light over the village, questioned Klaus about his plans and advised him to return home, which he said would be more pleasing to God than becoming a burden to strangers while Confederates were not always welcome beyond their own borders. Klaus took his leave and spent the night in the open under a hedge. If the course of events thus far was reminiscent of Abraham's experience of a heavenly injunction to "Stop!" and change direction, what happened next recalls St. Paul in a kind of Damascus Road experience.

As he later described it to Erny Rohrer and Heini am Grund, in a dream a shaft of light pierced and opened his belly like a knife. It was a painful and shattering experience and his earliest biographer adds that it was as if a rope were pulling him home. He was thus persuaded to go back to Obwalden in spite of the fact that his neighbours, who thought him a fool before, would now think him completely crazy. One writer has observed that God probably required Nicholas to experience the complete uncertainty of a man who, like Abraham, had accepted the leap of faith, in order to better understand that he would find no peace save through obedience alone. The dream had another strange consequence - from then on he lost all desire for food.

He retraced his steps and crept into his own hay-loft and slept for a few hours before moving on. How great the temptation would have been, upon seeing the light and movement in the house, to seek the warmth of his own hearth and the consolation of his beloved wife and family! He climbed high up the Klisterli Alp and remained for eight days without food in a nearly inaccessible place, "among the brambles and wild undergrowth," as Erny Rohrer later described it. He was then discovered by some hunters, among them his brother Peter, who was appalled by his emaciated appearance and implored him not to starve himself to death. He sent a message to the parish priest at Kerns, Oswald Isner, asking him to visit him. He told Isner that he had fasted for 11 days, and asked his advice, in confidence, whether he should begin eating again or continue the experiment. He said he had always longed to live without food and thus be more independent of the world. Isner related that after satisfying himself that the basis and justification of his fast was truly his love of God, he advised Klaus that he might try fasting still longer providing he could stand it without starving to death.

Word of his reappearance had spread and people flocked to his refuge, leaving him no peace. Then, as Erny Rohrer later recalled, Klaus "saw four bright lights in the sky which showed him the place where they should build him a dwelling and a chapel, which was done at his desire, according to the revelation he had received." With the aid of his neighbours, Klaus constructed a little hut and a year later, the Unterwaldiens, finally convinced of the authenticity of his vocation, built a chapel and a hermitage gratis. They still stand to this day, the hermitage consisting of two small rooms, one above the other, the upper room being Klaus' usual residence. The lower room contains a stove. The upper cell has a small window looking into the chapel; there he could contemplate Christ on the crucifix above the altar and follow the Holy Mass on those occasions when a priest was visiting. It is written in the earliest biography that the work was done in spite of opposition from some of Klaus' relations, who said that there should be more stringent proofs and a longer test period before hard-earned money and time were spent on the project. Such implied family criticism is consistent with the belief that Klaus' older sons did not really approve of his departure.

During his life, Klaus had already had several visions and dreams pointing him to The Ranft but it took this circuitous route before he finally settled there - about ten minutes walk from Flüe! However, despite this physical proximity, essential for his future role in the affairs of his country, Providence had simultaneously established a psychological distance and he never again crossed the threshold of his former home.

THE HOLY EUCHARIST: HIS ONLY FOOD

As news of the miraculous fast spread, Klaus' friends and neighbours in the canton were divided in their views, some accepting it and others suspecting a fraud. To determine the question definitively, the local authorities - including, no doubt, antagonistic officials exposed as corrupt by Klaus - organised a strict watch of all the approaches to Ranft and maintained it for a month with great severity until they were satisfied that no food was reaching him. It was some time after this that they built the chapel.

In order for the chapel to be consecrated, however, the episcopal authorities also needed to convince themselves about the matter of the fast. Bishop Hermann of Constance therefore sent his auxiliary, Bishop Thomas of Agathopolis, to investigate the situation. A draft of Bishop Herman's instructions still survive. He summarises the reports that had reached him from Unterwalden and, while recognising that anything is possible for God, wishes to protect those of simple faith from falling into "error and superstition" and therefore declares that one should *prudently* suspect "ambitious and fraudulent machinations" behind the alleged facts pertaining to Klaus. He continues:

"... according to the testimony of the apostles, the angels of darkness not infrequently transform themselves into angels of light and perform wonders that are not based on right foundations and should not be heeded...

Therefore we entrust to you, in your official capacity, as one in whom we have the greatest confidence, the

113

task of informing yourself exactly and in detail about the above-named circumstances, by private investigation and diligent examination... [asking you] to let us know as soon as possible whatever you find out that... seems to you to be proven or provable, so that we can make use of it for the spiritual health of the faithful.

Given in our palace at Constance in the year etc... under our episcopal seal which is attached to this letter."

On 27 April, 1469, Bishop Thomas visited The Ranft and in the course of a long conversation he quizzed Brother Klaus on religious matters. He asked Klaus what was the virtue most pleasing to God and when he replied: "Obedience," Thomas immediately produced the bread and wine he had specially brought for the purpose, broke the bread into three pieces and ordered Klaus to eat it. He did not want to disobey the Bishop's command, but he feared the difficulty of swallowing after such a long abstinence. He begged to be allowed to eat only one of the pieces but still struggled to swallow even that. Just one small sip of wine also caused him great pain. Much distressed, the Bishop declared that the test had satisfied him and that he had only insisted on it in obedience to the orders of his superior. The same day the chapel was consecrated. A year later the Church's approval was endorsed by a letter of perpetual indulgence signed by sixteen cardinals in Rome.

The technical term in Catholic theology for such a fast is *inedia*. While it is not uncommon among the saints and other blessed souls, Klaus' fast of twenty years - from October 1467 until his death in March 1487 - may be one of the longest unbroken periods. In the ten years from 1475, the fast, and its duration, were reported in chronicles or official records in the Palatinate, Austria, Gruyere and in his own district of Obwalden.

In her meticulously researched, short study, *Brother Klaus: Man of Two Worlds*, we find an outsider's assessment of this Catholic phenomenon. The author, Christina Yates, a Quaker, writes:

"Alongside the testimony of other people there is Brother Klaus' own attitude. The contemporary accounts of his character and personality make it even harder to imagine that he would have acquiesced in a 20-years' fraud, than to believe in the apparent miracle. When directly questioned about his fast he avoided a direct answer as far as possible. To Hans von Waldheim [an aristocrat who visited Klaus in May 1474 and recorded his impressions in detail] he just said 'God knows'... To an arrogant abbot who asked, 'Are you the one who boasts not to have eaten for so many years?' he replied, 'I have never said and I do not say, that I eat nothing.' He told the Dominican friar who visited him in 1469 that he had never revealed the answer to this 'difficult question to anyone except a pious priest from Lucerne' (Heini am Grund); under seal of secrecy he agreed to tell the friar, but the manuscript breaks off abruptly before reaching the critical point.

... two witnesses report him as directly referring to his fast. Erny Anderhalden testified that Klaus had told him more than once that God had granted him three great mercies among others: 'first that he obtained the agreement of his wife and children to his life as a hermit, secondly that he never had any wish, longing or temptation to return to his wife and children from his [hermit's] life and thirdly that he was able to live without bodily food or drink, as he [Anderhalden] firmly believed him to have done.'

In his statement in the Churchbook [of Sachseln], Oswald Isner, the parish priest of Kerns, recorded that: 'As Brother Klaus had perhaps been closer to him than to anyone else, and he had greatly wondered what kept him alive, he had often asked Brother Klaus and pressed him about it for a long time and once in his little house

Klaus had told him in great confidence that when he was present at Mass and the priest partook of the sacrament, he obtained a strength from this that enabled him to live without food or drink - otherwise he could not have borne it.'

These accounts of direct conversations with Brother Klaus seem to confirm that he was reluctant to discuss the matter, probably because he did not wish to seem to be claiming any special sanctity...

In the light of all the evidence available, Durrer [critical historian and biographer] concludes: 'If a purely historical question had been under discussion it would hardly have occurred to anyone to doubt these specific witnesses'."

Yates concludes:

"He means, of course, if the 'historical question' had not been a mind-boggling miracle. It was not accepted even in Brother Klaus' day without challenge and investigation by both the civil and religious authorities. But it *was* accepted and is an important element in his life which cannot be left out of the picture and quietly ignored... Catholic encyclopaedias record other more recent examples of what is technically called inedia..."

PRAYER AND MEDITATION

Beyond the uplifting pleasure to be found in the glorious natural surroundings of The Ranft, Klaus found the most profound joy in intimate, silent prayer. Some mystics of the time were attempting to attain union with God without the solid anchor of the Catholic faith. This lead them to pride and presumption. Brother Klaus always remained humble and completely submissive to the teachings of the Church. He considered humility as the fundamental disposition of the spiritual life. That was confirmed by the response made to John Geiler from Kaiserberg, a theological student and future preacher at Strasbourg Cathedral, who visited Ranft and asked Klaus if he did not fear taking a false path by devoting himself to a life and fast of such austerity. Nicholas replied: *"If I have humility and the Faith, I cannot take a false path."* It is again revealed in an account by a young man from Burgsdorf who later recalled that while talking with Klaus: "I said something more or less by chance which might have sounded like boasting, whereupon he, recognising the passion for righteousness which lay behind my words, said 'You should not boast of anything good in yourself'."

This humility and his deep attachment to the Catholic faith was probably due to his meditation on the life, passion and death of Jesus Christ, which nourished his religious thoughts and prayers. As already stated, Klaus could neither read nor write, but in those times reading was more than compensated for by frescoes and sculptures representing the mysteries of the Faith. Certain paintings still conserved in the Sachseln church and the church of St. Niklausen, the neighbouring hamlet to Flüe, helped Klaus throughout his life to penetrate the mysteries of salvation and they became for him a living reality.

Klaus was able to discuss the spiritual life with Brother Ulrich, a German who had made his way to Obwalden on foot and settled higher up on the river on the opposite bank of the Melchaa. Although very close to The Ranft, in keeping with rural areas where each field has its own identity, this place had a different name - Mösli. He had sought out Brother Klaus as a refuge for his soul from "the world [where] everything was so evil, sad, repulsive, bestial, bloody, barbaric and devilish and where the whole human race was a shameless pestilential band." In contrast to this despair and disgust with the human race, Brother Klaus, no stranger to sin and sorrow, did not dwell too much on moral judgements but taught Brother Ulrich of the joy to be found in a life of contemplation and self-discipline. Ulrich was an educated man who could read and write and no doubt discussed the gospels with Klaus and helped him with his correspondence.

In *Der Pilgertrakt* (Pilgrim's tractate or treatise), the earliest printed work in which Brother Klaus is named, the anonymous author - who just describes himself as a "respectable pilgrim" - indulges in a theological dialogue with Klaus. The visit probably took place between 1469 and 1477 but the little book appeared at least ten years later, in three editions published in 1487-88. Only a small portion of the 21 page text directly quotes the hermit but at one point the writer states, as summarised in part by Yates:

"Then I said that if he didn't mind I should like to discuss something else. He answered, 'Speak!' So I continued. 'When we ask God for our daily bread, what is this bread?' He replied, 'You speak first!'

They went on to discuss the difference between natural or earthly bread, available to all God's creatures, and the sacramental bread, and the Pilgrim gives the last word to Brother Klaus:

'Then almighty God mysteriously enters the tiny Host and this is transformed, so that henceforth it is no longer earthly bread, but flesh and blood, with unspeakable grace, true God and true man, invisible. And in every Host that has been blessed by the priest, the Godhead abides, whole and complete. Here you have my interpretation'."

Also discussed was a picture of a wheel that Klaus meditated upon in seeking to understand the Holy Trinity and which today, together with a painting called the "Meditation-Picture" apparently based on the wheel diagram, forms an integral part of the study of Brother Klaus' spirituality. For the first time the Pilgrim gives the initiative to Klaus:

"Next Brother Klaus said, 'If you don't mind I'd like

to show you my 'book' which I am studying, seeking to understand it's teaching.' Then he produced a drawing of a diagram like a wheel with six spokes, as shown here:

"He went on to say, 'Do you see this figure? This is the Divine Being. The centre represents the undivided Godhead, in which all the saints rejoice. The three pointed ends entering the inner ring represent the three Persons. They have proceeded from the single Godhead and embraced Heaven and the whole world. Here - they go outwards in divine power and here they return and are one and undivided in eternal sovereignty. That is what this figure means.'

Brother Klaus developed his meditation on the wheel in relation to the Visitation of Mary by the Holy Ghost, the Eucharist and the way to Eternity.

Of the Eucharist he said:

'Now see this spoke, which likewise is broad at the central ring and narrow at the outer ring - in this way the great power of the almighty God is contained in the tiny substance of the Host.'

Of the way to Eternity:

'Now observe this spoke also - this too is broad at the centre and narrow towards the outer ring. It represents the value of our life, which is altogether small and perishable. In the brief time (of our life on earth) through God's love we can gain unspeakable joy, which never comes to an end. That is the meaning of my wheel.' "These words (writes the pilgrim) rejoiced my heart. This was the speech he addressed to me."

Brother Klaus asked the Pilgrim what he thought about a visitation like the plague. Can a man escape this wrath? The Pilgrim said he would answer as well as he could. He quoted from the Book of Ezekiel, how a man clothed in linen and bearing an inkhorn marked those who were to be spared because of their righteousness, and he (the Pilgrim) thought that those who are spared are spared according to God's will.

"Brother Klaus looked at me open-mouthed. 'That is entirely my view - that no one can escape the wrath of God, but the man who remains in the truth and lives in the love of God - with him all will be well.'

The Pilgrim then expressed his conviction that the man who held fast to truth, had confidence in God and recognised that God Himself is locked and secured in the noble queen, Maria, would never be overcome.

"With some such words I took leave of him and... he embraced me and said, 'God grant you health and happiness'."

The dialogue evokes a delightful image of the two holy men in deep and protracted discussion about these and many other aspects of the Faith.

THE VISIONS

With regard to their discourse on the wrath of God, it should be mentioned that Klaus himself had seen it in one of his many visions. According to Wölflin, people visiting Brother Klaus were "overcome with terror at first sight of him. He himself gave as the reason that he had once seen an enormous blaze of light surrounding a human countenance, and at the sight of it his heart was shattered and he was seized with terror. Completely stunned, he instinctively turned his eyes away and fell to the ground. For this reason his own looks now appeared terrifying to other people." Other reports seem to indicate that he did not retain this appearance for the rest of his life. Nonetheless, a French priest and theologian, Charles de Bouelles who visited Ranft in 1503 and stayed with one of Klaus' sons, confirmed in a letter to a friend that Klaus had indeed seen "the image of a human head with a frightful expression, full of wrath and menace."

As it happens, this particular vision was of special interest to C.G. Jung. Though steeped in the occult himself and no friend of Catholicism, Jung held Brother Klaus in high esteem - referring to him as "My Brother Klaus." Regarding the visions generally, Jung dismisses the average sceptic with this biting passage: "I am a good deal less sophisticated than the so-called educated public whose philosophical embarrassment is such that it sighs with relief when visions are equated with hallucinations, delusional ideas, mania and schizophrenia, or whatever else these morbid things may be called, and are reduced to the right denominator by some competent authority."

Within the confines of this summary it is not possible to provide the full transcript of the visions and consider them in detail. Nonetheless, in addition to those already mentioned in passing, the following brief overview still provides a marvellous glimpse of the spiritual life of a soul specially chosen by God from eternity, bearing in mind the words of St. John Chrysostom: "To some the grace was imparted through dreams, to others it was openly poured forth. For indeed by dreams the prophets saw, and received revelations."

One of the strangest of his "memories" was confided to his friend Fr. Heini am Grund who relates that Klaus had told him that:

"In his mother's womb, before he was born, he had seen a star in the sky that shone over the whole world and since he had lived in The Ranft he had constantly seen a star like it in the sky, so that he firmly believed that this star was himself... Brother Klaus also told him that before his birth, in his mother's womb... he saw a great stone, which meant the steadiness and constancy with which he should persevere. And at the same time, in his mother's womb, he saw the Holy Oil and when he was born and came into the world he had recognised his mother and the midwife and saw himself being carried through The Ranft to Kerns with such clarity that he... still saw it today as well as when it actually happened. At the same time he saw an old man standing by the font whom he didn't know, but the priest who baptised him, Klaus knew quite well."

As well as intimating that a special path lay ahead, visions also reminded him that he was in danger of straying from the narrow path of salvation. Wölflin describes the most memorable:

"One day, when he went to the pasture to see his cattle, he sat down on the ground and began as was his way to pray in the depths of his being and to give himself up to divine contemplation. Suddenly he saw coming from his own mouth a white lily of wondrous scent which went up towards heaven. But just then his cattle (from whose yield he supported the whole family) came past. For a moment he looked away, fastening his gaze on one horse that was the finest of them all. Then he saw the lily bend down over the horse and get completely eaten up by the animal as it passed. Taught by this vision, he recognised that the treasure that is to be kept back for heaven cannot be found by those thirsting for earthly possessions, and that the gifts of heaven, if they are mingled with the cares and interests of this earthly life, will be choked just like the seed of the word of God that sprang up among thorns."

Wölflin describes another occasion (also briefly mentioned by Klaus' son Walter) when God spoke to him out of a cloud saying that he was a "foolish man" if he thought that in his own strength, and unwillingly, he could submit to God's will, for willing obedience was what God wanted: "Warned by this voice he began to disregard the domestic interests over which until now he had taken such great pains, and instead to devote himself with more care than ever to heavenly matters." This probably happened not long before the break.

His experience of the village of Liestal lit up in flames and the ensuing mystical experiences that caused him to return to Obwalden, also seem to belong to this category of guidance and warning.

Finally, there are several other longer, detailed visions, related in the original texts in a naive, primitive style as if they were the direct words of St. Nicholas himself. One of them, "The Heavenly Quaternity," is in large part related to Dorothy by Klaus in Part I of *The Invisible Crown*. The other two, known as "The Singing Pilgrim" and "The Fountain," are simply told yet profound and repay thoughtful reading, as the following extract reveals:

The Singing Pilgrim

"It seemed to him in his spirit there came a man dressed in pilgrim fashion... And when the traveller came up to the man he stood before him and sang these words: Alleluia. And when he began to sing his voice resounded, and everything between heaven and earth rang in sympathy as the small organ pipes support the big ones. And he heard three perfect (complete) words issuing from one source; they were then shut away again as if behind a lock with a powerful spring. And after he had heard the three perfect words none of which had touched either of the others, he still wanted to talk only of one... And behold (the traveller) was transformed... such a splendid, well-formed man that he could not do anything but gaze upon him with undisguised joy and longing... the traveller turned his eyes on him. And then many great miracles took place: Mount Pilatus sank into the ground and the whole world was open to him so that it seemed as if all the sins in the world were made known to him. And there appeared a great crowd of people, and behind the people the Truth appeared, but they all had their faces turned away from the Truth. And every one of them had a great growth on his heart, as big as two fists. And this growth was selfishness, which led the people so greatly astray that they could not bear the sight of the traveller any more than one can bear the heat of fiery flames, and in terrible fear they turned round and went back with great abuse and outrage. From far off he could see them disappearing. But the Truth behind their backs - that stayed there. Then the traveller's face changed and became like the face of Christ on Veronica's veil, and the man had a great longing to see more of him... (when the traveller) bowed to the man and took leave of him... (he) was aware that there was such love in the traveller towards him that he was overwhelmed, for he knew that he did not deserve this love... And he saw in his spirit that his face and his eyes and his whole body were as full of loving humility as a pot filled with honey till it cannot hold another drop... (and) he was so utterly satisfied by him that he desired nothing further from him. It seemed to him that the traveller had revealed everything to him that was in heaven and upon earth."

THE COVENANT OF STANS

The regular and creative contribution of this solitary mystic to political affairs, represents nothing less than the antithesis of that *exaggerated* separation of Church and State so dogmatically entrenched in modern democracies. To those enamoured of this view that religious belief is a private domain with no place in the public forum - a godless idea rooted in a godless, anti-Catholic bloodbath known as *la Revolution française* - St. Nicholas von Flüe must be an aberration! Not only were his views frequently sought on "international" matters, but he has earned a permanent place in Swiss history for his decisive, peace-making role in the internal conflicts and constitutional crisis that followed the Burgundy War (1475-77) and were settled by the Covenant of Stans in 1481. Some knowledge of the years leading up to the settlement is necessary to really appreciate the importance and value of his contribution.

By the mid-14th century, the three original cantons (in those days simply called *Orte* - "places") - Uri, Schwyz and Unterwalden - had been joined by five more: Lucerne, Zurich, Glarus, Zug and Berne. They signed two agreements that marked the beginning of the common legislation of the embryo Confederation: The "Pastor's Ordinance" (1370), regulating the relationship between the Church and secular authorities and safeguarding traffic, particularly on the St. Gotthard route to the south; and the Covenant of Sempach (1393) which established minimum standards of military discipline in an effort to stop wanton butchery and protect non-combatants. Then developed various regional pacts and overlapping networks of alliances and administration both between cantons and with immediate neighbours beyond the Confederation. The whole parliament (Diet) was thus required to meet regularly to receive and discuss reports and this fostered a sense of unity and common purpose between the Confederates.

There were, however, tensions between the three original rural cantons and the cities. These were not just the result of a certain arrogant assumption of leadership roles by the cities or economic differences between farmers and powerful city guilds. The form of government and source of authority were also different in the mountainous rural cantons where, instead of a city aristocracy, the community leaders were independent farmers whose forefathers had fought to free themselves from outside domination. Decisions were made in open-air meetings *(Landsgemeinde)*. There was less concentration of power in a few hands, less scope for decisions behind closed doors. The rural cantons were thus very sympathetic to country folk living in areas belonging to the cities, who were little better than serfs, and when they rebelled the rural cantons secretly or even openly sympathised with them. Occupying central territory, they were also in a different position regarding foreign policy. Hemmed in by the other cantons, they could only expand their territory southwards and they fiercely protected this southern border.

For their part, the cities pursued expansionist policies in a mixture of foreign alliances that lead to all kinds of contradictions - such as Berne supporting Freiburg and Solothurn but siding with the rural cantons against Lucerne in certain questions. They also felt that the lack of discipline throughout the country regions threatened the stability of the Confederation. This disorder escalated in the second half of the 15th century following the victory, in alliance with Louis XI of France, against Charles the Bold of Burgundy. The frugal, hardworking farmers of the Forest Cantons acquired wealth beyond their dreams when in 1477, at the Battle of Nancy, Charles the Bold was killed and the enormous treasure he took with him on his campaigns - articles in gold and silver and precious jewellery - was captured by the Swiss. With it came a veritable poisoning of their spiritual lives. Already simmering vices such as greed and jealousy were inflamed to unprecedented levels and reached an all time low with the antics of a group which, as Yates observes, might today have been labelled the "Crazy Gang!"

In the Spring of 1477, a group of disgruntled ex-soldiers from the three original Forest Cantons gathered together and railed against the cities in general, who they accused of pocketing all the Burgundian gold, and the men of Geneva in particular, who had not paid them money promised after the 1475 campaign in Vaud. They set off to collect their debts, gathering forces on the way and marching under a banner bearing a pig and a village idiot carrying a purse and club! They called themselves the "Company of the Mad Life." Looting and pillaging as they went, their numbers had swelled to about 2,000 by the time they reached Freiburg. Here they were halted by gifts of wine and cash and a promise of a final settlement with Geneva.

This breakdown of law and order so alarmed the city-states that in May 1477 Berne, Zurich and Lucerne signed an agreement *(Ewiges Burgrecht)* with Freiburg and Solothurn which in effect took precedence over the agreements and pacts already existing between the three cities and the five rural cantons. This particularly embittered the relationship between Lucerne and the three other Forest Cantons, whose previous majority (five rural cantons, three cities) was now threatened by their influential neighbour joining forces with four other cities, two of them non-members of the Confederation. The cities desired more centralised authority and inter-cantonal arrangements to control rebellious subjects. The rural cantons wanted as much independence as possible and to retain their previously enjoyed influence.

This was the complicated background to the long-standing difficulties solved by the Covenant of Stans. As Brother Klaus prayed and fasted, the Confederation beyond The Ranft was suffering from discord of every kind, full of confusions and contradictions and inadequate machinery for dealing with them. In the several years leading up to Stans, friendly mediation, legal proceedings and arbitration sought to settle these internal differences, especially over the *Burgrecht* agreement between Lucerne and the four cities, Berne and Zurich (within the Confederation) and Freiburg and Solothurn (outside it). Regular interruptions in the form of wars and complications with a host of foreign powers and allies, only served to confirm the urgent need for internal cohesion in the face of such external pressures.

During these years, Brother Klaus was kept informed of the situation through visits by state officials and there seems little doubt that he influenced the thinking of the men who produced a series of draft documents leading up to a meeting of the Diet held in Stans in November 1481. After a difficult round of negotiations the delegates returned to their cantons for further instructions. When they returned in mid-December, the atmosphere was heavy and the Diet became a battlefield of intransigence and recriminations. On 21 December it dissolved in fierce disagreement and the delegates returned to their lodgings and prepared for departure the following day, convinced that only force of arms could solve their problems. The people were seized with terror by the prospect of a bloody civil war that would obliterate their nearly 200 year old Confederation.

The only eyewitness account of the events on 22 December is by Diebold Schilling, who accompanied his father, the official scribe who actually penned the final agreement. He was 21 at the time and his account was written 25 years later in the course of his "Lucerne Chronicle," a general history of the period:

> "At this time an upright and pious priest was in charge of the church at Stans, Herr Heini am Grund by name, a native of Lucerne, who was very dear to Brother Klaus in The Ranft. This Herr Heini knew enough to realise that nothing but war could result. He got up in the night and hastened to Brother Klaus [a distance of ten miles] and described the situation to him at such length that [meanwhile] the disputants were at their wits' end, and

in the afternoon everyone was planning to go home and do his best to make ready, for no one could see any outcome but war. When they had eaten and were ready to depart Herr Heini came running from Brother Klaus, rushed everywhere into the inns and with tears in his eyes begged the deputies for the sake of God and Brother Klaus to assemble again and hear Brother Klaus' advice and opinion. This was done, but the message he brought was not made known to everyone, for Brother Klaus had forbidden Herr Heini to reveal it to anyone but the deputies. And so God granted the happy result; bad as it had been in the morning, through this message things became [so] much better [that] within an hour everything was settled and disposed of. My father... was immediately ordered to record in writing the agreement he had previously drafted, and this was then done as quickly as possible. Freiburg and Solothurn were included in this agreement... and the Burgrecht question was settled... This caused universal rejoicing..."

Yates writes that "the dramatic change in atmosphere affected not only the urgent question of signing the two documents but also the sorting out of loose ends not formally dealt with on that day [including a formula for settling the dispute over the Burgundy booty]... it provided a basis for the development of the Confederation for more than 300 years... All accounts agree that it was his [Brother Klaus'] last-minute intervention that saved the Confederation at the critical moment. However important his counsels may have been during the years of rumbling disagreement, a clear lead at the moment of deadlock, from a man of great spiritual authority, was seized upon with eagerness... The role of Heini am Grund was also crucial. Providentially he had become parish priest at Stans in the previous June... In 1981 the route he took through the snow on that winter night 500 years earlier was made into a pedestrian pilgrim's way and a memorial stone was unveiled in Stans to mark the starting point."

A number of letters have survived describing the subsequent rejoicing, bell-ringing and the like and expressing gratitude to Brother Klaus. The Mayor and Council of Solothurn sent a letter of thanks and a book to Heini am Grund and enclosed 20 guilders to be passed on to Brother Klaus for a perpetual Mass for a year. To Brother Klaus himself they wrote:

"We have been informed that by the grace of God and his dear Mother you have achieved peace, quiet and concord by your faithful counsel and guidance. And that you spoke so much good on our behalf that we are now joined in brotherhood and a permanent union with the whole Confederation. For that we can fairly give great praise and thanks to the true God and the whole heavenly host and to you as a lover of peace..."

Despite the clearly providential and pivotal role of a man of God in bringing down Communism in recent times, a fact admitted by Gorbachev himself about John Paul II, it must seem incomprehensible to the age in which we live that a "parliament" would even listen to, let alone act upon the advice of a simple hermit. But if men and women of the pre-Reformation Middle Ages lacked the modern, secular gods of democracy and technology, they all shared one priceless treasure. Despite their grave faults and their greed and grasping, despite their warlike disposition and social differences, the Confederates were profoundly Catholic - bound together, in spite of themselves, by the universality and unifying "authority" principle of Catholicism. They recognised God as the sole arbiter of their destiny and His Commandments, interpreted and taught by His Church, as the only basis for lasting peace. They knew well that at the heart of their disputes lay a turning away from these fundamental principles.

In Brother Klaus, therefore, they approached a man having renounced wealth, power, honour and all the earthly things that were the source of their own divisions; an obedient son of Holy Mother Church who sought God alone and the accomplishment of His Will. They knew that Klaus would find the solution through prayer and dialogue with the Lord. In his advice they recognised the Will of God and knew that the blessing of Heaven accompanied his intervention. This blessing is manifested in the Switzerland of today which unites such culturally diverse cantons in a way that must seem miraculous to countries incessantly torn by fratricidal civil wars. Since the Reformation, Brother Klaus has been venerated by both Catholic and Protestant Switzerland as the guide and protector of Swiss peace and neutrality.

From the time of the admission of Freiburg and Solothurn, neutrality was understood as a creative principle of effective peace-making rather than a selfish desire to keep out of trouble. In *Waging Peace*, William Lloyd, an American student of the Swiss phenomenon, notes that newly-joined members of the Confederation were obliged to pledge themselves not to take sides in inter-cantonal disputes and to act as mediators if required. From this point of view the idea of neutrality is implicit in the Covenant of Stans and is an attempt to give substance to Brother Klaus' insistence that *"Peace is always in God."*

The first explicit reference to Brother Klaus' advice to adopt neutrality as a general principle of foreign policy appears in an account of his life by the German historian Trithemius, writing twenty-five years after the hermit's death. It runs as follows:

"O dear friends, don't make your fence too wide, the better to remain in peace, calm and unity in your honourable and hard won liberty. Don't burden yourselves with foreign affairs, don't join up with foreign rulers, guard against dissension and self-seeking. Protect your fatherland and cleave to it. Do not foster intentional love of fighting, but if anyone attacks you, then fight bravely for freedom and fatherland."

GUIDE AND COMFORTER

Life in The Ranft became even more hectic after Stans and Klaus' habit of prayer and meditation between sunrise and midday was frequently disturbed by pilgrims and official visitors. He would often seek refuge in the deepest part of the forest to complete his spiritual duties. Although far less accessible than it is today, the little chapel in The Ranft was often besieged by people from the Confederation and elsewhere. Reminiscent of twentieth century crowds who flocked to Franciscan stigmatist Padre Pio in Italy, they had to wait their turn to see the hermit. Many were no doubt motivated by curiosity but many others sought counsel on serious spiritual, professional or political problems. According to the testimony of the day he was a clear and confident counsellor in matters of life and Catholic morals and entirely faithful to the doctrines of the Church. "He had a particular gift not only to encourage simple souls," wrote Trithemius, "but also to console those who were sad and demoralised, a gift that Divine Power had conferred on him in view of the utter purity of his heart."

Apart from spiritual consolation people also reported miraculous physical cures, but above all we have a consistent picture of a man possessing great love of neighbour, wisdom and a desire to serve and help others - sometimes, like Padre Pio, aided by supernatural gifts such as clairvoyance. One very distressed woman, from the neighbouring village of Kerns, was convinced that her husband was being unfaithful and fearing that she might kill the woman involved came to seek Brother Klaus' advice. She found so many people in the chapel and going in and out of his cell that she thought she may as well go home. As she was about to leave the chapel, Brother Klaus entered and said to the crowd: "There is a woman here who wants my advice. She can go in peace. Her suspicions are unjust. The couple are innocent." Having said this, he returned to his cell.

In another memorable encounter with a young man from Burgdorf, who later recorded the event, he is consulted about a practical decision and a spiritual one and provides assistance with both. On his first visit to Ranft, a journey of 2-3 days from Burgdorf, the young man asked Klaus if it would be alright to remain in Ranft and serve God, although his parents knew nothing of his intention and his conscience was not clear. Klaus answered him: "If you intend to serve God, you must pay no heed to anyone. But if you just think it would be nice to spend your days here then you would do better to stay with your own folk, and support them." He went away satisfied but returned again at a later date, having decided to serve God, and after discussing with Klaus the sort of Order he might join his "doubts were set at rest." Klaus was seated on a "heap of stones," the young man sitting at his feet:

"Then I asked him another question. 'In what way should a man contemplate Christ's Passion? Should he imagine the suffering Christ actually present before his eyes and suffer with Him, as if it were his brother, or should he think of the Passion as something in the past, in the sense that Christ has already overcome it all and reigns in glory, and rejoice with Him that now all is well and all those tortures are over?' He replied, 'Whichever way you follow is good.' And he added, 'For God can make a man's contemplation as delightful as going to a dance, or just the opposite, it's as if he were fighting a battle.' When he spoke of dancing, I looked at him as if I were a little shocked that a man like him should talk of dancing. He immediately noticed this and repeated the expression: *'Ja, als solt er an dantz gon.'*

133

"Then I complained to him of my failure to persist in the good life, how I did not stick to my good resolution but at the very first opportunity my desire would turn once more to the forbidden thing, so that I would be separated from God, as before. He replied that one had to rise up again quickly."

St. Nicholas was very well informed about complex political affairs both at home and abroad and as Yates suggests: "Perhaps the very fact that he was not assaulted by all kinds of sophisticated media (as we are today) enabled him to see general principles more clearly... he could think objectively and see beyond narrow local interests." After a special envoy of the Duke of Milan, Bernadino Imperiali, had spent an evening and a morning with him discussing a protracted and dangerous dispute between several cantons and the Duke over customs duties, he wrote a lengthy report to his ducal employer, stating:

"The Confederates have great confidence in him. I found him informed about the whole thing... The affair grieved him sorely and he prayed God would make peace. As I knew that his son was Landamman of Unterwalden I asked the hermit to explain the situation to him... He said he would send a message in writing to be read at the next Council Meeting... The hermit asked me to give his greetings and regards to your Excellency... and assured me of his sincere love for you and begged you to overlook minor matters in order to live in peace with the Confederates."

The matter was resolved, war averted and Imperiali returned home. During the years 1480-83 his visitors also included messengers from the Habsburg Archduke Sigmund of Austria, who brought a gift of 100 guilders for the chapel and the secretary of two Italian counts with a letter of introduction from the authorities in Berne.

With money from the likes of the Archduke Sigmund, the

authorities in Lucerne and Solothurn as well as the donations made at the chapel, Klaus was able to set up an endowment that made possible the appointment of a permanent chaplain for the chapel in October 1482. This meant the frequent celebration of Holy Mass, which Klaus was able to follow from the small window looking down into the chapel from his cell.

In December the authorities in Berne sent Brother Klaus a gift of 40 pounds for the chapel. After thanking the donors for their generous gift, he continues:

"I will write more. Obedience is the greatest glory that there is in heaven and on earth and therefore you must strive to be obedient to each other; and wisdom is the most valuable for it is the starting point of all things. Peace is in God always, for God is peace and peace should not be disturbed. Where there is unrest peace will be disturbed. See to it therefore that peace is what you stand on, protect widows and orphans as you have done till now.

Avoid public wrong-doing and always stand by righteousness. You must also keep in your hearts God's Passion, for it is man's greatest comfort in his last moments. Many people are in a state of doubt about their Faith and the devil makes many attacks on faith - above all in this matter of faith. We must not be in any doubt, for the Faith is as it has been revealed. And I do not write this to you because I think you do not believe as you should. I do not doubt that you are good Christians. I write as a warning so that if the evil spirit should attack you you may resist with knightly valour.

That is all. God be with you. Given on St. Martin's Day [4th December] in the year 82. At the end of this letter I have affixed my own seal.

I Brother Klaus"

This letter has been called Brother Klaus' "political testament" as it is the nearest thing we have to a general statement on political matters in his own words. Peace is a by-product of obedience to God because *peace is always in God.* Perhaps it is best summed up in what is regarded as Brother Klaus' fundamental political maxim:

"What the soul is to the body, God is to the State. When the soul leaves the body, the body falls apart. When God is driven from the State, the State is doomed to ruin."

There are also two detailed reports of visits to Brother Klaus written by an aristocrat from North Germany, Hans von Waldheim, who visited in May 1474, and a cleric, Dean Albrecht von Bonstetten, who arrived on 31 December 1478. Von Waldheim describes a meeting with Dorothy [he underestimates Dorothy's age, as she was certainly more than 40]:

"...the priest asked me if I would like to see Brother Klaus' wife as well. I said yes. He showed me a house on an airy hilltop across a deep valley and said that was where Brother Klaus used to live and where his wife and youngest son still lived; the older sons, who were already married, lived not far off. He said to the boat boy: 'Run over to Brother Klaus' wife and tell her I'll be holding Mass and if they want to hear it she should come and bring the youngest boy along with her.'

We went on and reached Brother Klaus' cell... The priest went to the altar and looked up the office for St. Mary Magdalena and when he had found it he turned round and saw Brother Klaus' wife and son. I gave her and the boy my hand and wished them good morning. His wife is still a good-looking young woman of under 40, fresh faced with a smooth skin. I asked her 'Dear lady, how long has Brother Klaus been gone?' She replied, 'This boy here, my son, will be seven years old on St. John the Baptist Day [24th June] and when he was 13 weeks old - it was on St. Gallus' Day - Brother Klaus parted from me and he has never been with me since.' I had quite a lot more talk with her and the son. The boy has an upright carriage like Brother Klaus and he is the image of his father."

Of Klaus, Dean von Bonstetten wrote:

"The servant of God awaited us in the upper part [of the cell] and when he saw us he spoke softly and modestly in a manly voice, barefoot, upright: 'Greetings to you beloved Fathers and Brothers in God,' and gave us his hand in correct fashion. We thanked him, all quite overcome, and really my hair stood on end and my voice failed me. He went on, 'Why have you come to this remote gorge in this wild place? Just so that you could see me, a poor sinner? I am afraid you will find nothing in me worthy of a visit from such people as you.' ... We asked him about various things and he answered not as if trying to make an impression but in general as befitted an unlearned but exceptional and outstanding man, so that he would have compelled respect even from an enemy. I had a good look around to take everything in and to observe exactly his person and the room. He is tall, very thin, brown and wrinkled, with uncombed hair, black mixed with grey, not very thick. His beard is about a thumb's length, he has medium-sized eyes, with very clear whites, well preserved teeth and a nose that goes well with his face. He is not talkative, and reserved with strangers... He is bareheaded and barefoot and wears nothing on his bare body but a grey robe... I saw no domestic utensils, no table or bed on which the servant of God could have lain. He has to stand or sit, or lie on the floor of the little room, if he wants to rest."

FINAL YEARS AND LEGACY

As the influx of visitors continued, Brother Klaus was more and more troubled by various demands made upon him and by disputatious priests and others who plagued him with severe, impromptu examinations. In a letter to the authorities in Lucerne seeking checks and curbs on those foreign visitors coming to The Ranft, the Landamman of Obwalden stated that "one foreign priest, when he could not confound him, uttered threats, and announced he would put someone else on to him who would have to test and examine him even more rigorously."

A few years later, in a curious sequel to this disputatious priest, a certain abbot from a monastery in Germany, accompanied by a fellow abbot, visited Brother Klaus and raised the old familiar controversies. As recorded by the historian Trithemius:

"The hermit replied to everything precisely and modestly, without the slightest sign of impatience, although he was being hard pressed by the abbot, who was determined to 'get to the bottom' of Brother Klaus and his beliefs. Among other questions he asked: 'Are you the one who boasts not to have eaten for so many years?' The hermit replied: 'Good Father, I have never said and do not say, that I eat nothing.' The abbot persisted and, in the hope of provoking the mild-mannered old man, led the conversation round to covetousness and asked him: 'What is avarice?'

Then Brother Klaus struck:

'Why do you ask me, an uneducated man who owns nothing, about avarice, when you learned and rich as you are, not only know better than I do, but have had personal experience of what goes on in an avaricious man's heart? The year before last, in a craze for speculation, you brought 27 measures of best wine for a

138

derisory price and then last year resold it for a huge profit. But your Bishop confounded your cupidity and through his own greed punished yours; in spite of your protests he seized the whole lot by force...and removed it to his own cellar and didn't pay a penny for it and never will. The marks of greed are written on your face and are rooted in your heart and to your mortification have now become obvious.'

At these words the abbot was dumbfounded and confused and did not reply."

Trithemius said that he got this delightful story direct from the other abbot. He confirms that Brother Klaus' accusation was factually correct, but cannot imagine how the hermit in his remote valley could possibly have known of the transaction unless by direct revelation through the Holy Spirit. Writing not long after the event Trithemius did not give the abbot's name, but historical research later identified him.

Despite the behaviour of such clergy and earlier mentioned tensions within his own Sachseln parish that continued throughout his lifetime, Klaus remained in total awe of the Priesthood of Jesus Christ and the supernatural power conferred on Catholic priests at ordination. A Dominican friar who visited "the pious and devout Brother Nikolaus of Flu (sic) in Unterwalden on Corpus Christi day and the Friday following [8th and 9th June] in the year 1469," reported that in the course of relating some facts of his earlier life, Klaus stated:

"... of all humankind I most valued and honoured the royal and priestly folk - that is to say Christ's priests, so that whenever I saw a priest it was as if I saw one of God's angels. It was first through this, I think, that I came to hold in such reverence and honour the Blessed Sacrament of the Body and Blood of Jesus Christ."

Clearly, the disquiet in the Church of his time - populated by the same worldly churchmen who beset our own scandal-ridden age

- did not shake Klaus' faith. He could not escape talk about the latest scandals and it is likely that he even witnessed clerical transgressions at The Ranft. He was also asked to assist in resolving the sordid affair of the Convent of Klingental, which started as a matter of religious discipline and ended in a serious political dispute. But as all this raged around him, Klaus remained fixed and undisturbed in the same vision of the Church and the priesthood that had sustained him from childhood days. His attitude in this regard is attested to in the biography by Heini Gundelfingen, his contemporary, who wrote:

> "Through his salutary and thoroughly practical exhortations, he led his compatriots to fear God and observe His Commandments. He asked them to follow the teachings of their priests, even if they did not give good example. He illustrated his discourse with this beautiful allegory: 'If a fountain has several pipes - pipes of lead, copper, silver and gold, they still dispense the same water; likewise, we can receive the same grace from good and bad priests who administer the Sacrament of the Eucharist, providing we are worthy of it'."

His own peace-making spirit with the troublesome clergy in Sachseln is perhaps seen in his giving them the two six-foot high bronze candlesticks sent to him by Bishop Hermann of Constance after the consecration of his chapel. Not that it had much effect - as late as 1484 there was yet another outbreak of trouble with the incumbent of Sachseln!

By this time, however, Klaus was withdrawing more into the background and his name is not linked with political matters towards the end of his life. This may well be connected to his sons' growing influence in political affairs, some of whose activities would have caused both he and Dorothy considerable distress. Hans, now in his mid-thirties, was elected to the high position of *Landamman* in Obwalden. He was accused of complicity in a plot against the foreign city of Landau, and although the evidence implicating him was obtained under torture the episode must have grieved the old hermit. In the publicity surrounding the affair Hans von Flüe is frequently described as "Brother Klaus' son." Neither Hans nor Walter were in sympathy with their father's position on the question of foreign levies (the "pensions") and probably not with his far-seeing and unparochial attitude to constitutional matters. Walter and his son and grandson, both called Nicholas, also rose to the high office of *Landamman*. Walter actually married Barbara Anderhalden, the daughter of his father's life-long friend, Erny, and it is from Walter that most of the very many von Flüe families living today have descended. At the time of the hermit's death, the young Nicholas was studying theology in Paris and there are some delightful stories of the rapport he maintained with his father while abroad.

Few details are known of his last illness. He suffered acute pain in all his limbs and because of extreme emaciation could find no way to lie in comfort. It is surmised and one hopes that Dorothy was permitted to nurse him at the end. In one fictional account, to her whispered request to remain he replies: "Surely God would allow us this last mercy." On the eighth day of his illness he asked for Holy Viaticum and after receiving the Precious Body and Blood of Christ with the greatest respect, stretched out on the floor of his cell, he gave up his soul. It was his seventieth birthday, 21 March 1487.

News of the death travelled fast and a huge crowd attended his funeral in Sachseln. All the neighbouring churches were closed so that their parish priests could attend. His remains were firstly laid in the churchyard. Today, encased in gold, they lie in front of the altar in the 17th century church.

The procedure for beatification commenced in 1591 but due to various circumstances and the strict procedures and legal form required by the Church, he was not declared blessed until 1669 by Pope Clement IX. It was not until 15 May, 1947, that the hermit was canonised by Pope Pius XII. In his allocution he spoke of a saint sent by Divine Providence for the needs of our time, and added: *"Wherever we encounter Nicholas von Flüe, we see in him a man filled with the fear of God."* The Holy Father was referring, of course, to the filial and loving fear of God that is both the beginning of wisdom and an ever *constructive* social force which, according to John Paul II, "creates holy men and women - true Christians - to whom the future of the world ultimately belongs."

Today, although accessible by car and possessing three hotels, Flüeli is relatively unspoilt. In the centre of the village both the timber house where Klaus was born and the house where he raised his family have been preserved in their 15th century state. The Ranft itself can be reached only by foot. A steep path leads down to the chapel and hermitage where the peaceful surroundings have barely changed in 500 years. A larger chapel, built in 1501 about a hundred metres lower down by the Melchaa, remains a place of pilgrimage in times of crisis. In 1914 and again in 1939 thousands of pilgrims flocked there to pray for their country and for the world.

Given the broad appeal of this extraordinary Catholic, it is perhaps not surprising that the only scholarly work on his life available in English was the small piece written by non-Catholic, Christina Yates [RIP]. As the major source for this brief introduction to the life and world of Brother Klaus, it is appropriate to add her final ecumenical reflections on the hermit from Ranft:

> "Brother Klaus stands for a radically different scale of values, and jolts people into questioning the purposes of life. Is material success the only yardstick? What do men and women really need? What is the meaning of true simplicity? What does love of country demand of its citizens? Are there higher loyalties? No one accuses a man of deserting his family if he leaves them to defend

his homeland. Nicholas of Flüe was aware, in a way that most men are not aware, of another world to which his ultimate loyalty was pledged, a mysterious world which he spent his life exploring and making real to others...

...His advice was rooted in common sense and stemmed from reflection on the practical problems of everyday life and human relationships as well as from the contemplation which leaves earthly things behind. Illiteracy in the Middle Ages was not necessarily a sign of lack of intelligence... Within himself Brother Klaus possessed a compass which unerringly sought the true direction, and showed when to compromise and when to stand firm. This inward compass led him into the world of eternal values which to him was so real, and back again into the earthly country where most of his fellow men and women spent their lives. There was no contradiction in this - the things he perceived with his inward eye and with his physical sight were parts of one coherent whole. This undivided man has a message for our divided world."

The essence of that message and the key to Brother Klaus' undivided world - *one*, *coherent*, and *whole* - is **obedience to the truth**: to God and His Commandments as taught by His Holy Church of Rome. As long as ostensibly Christian societies reject that prerequisite and its attendant ramifications, they will continue to search in vain for *genuine* solutions to the alienation, divisions and social crises draining the joy of life from their people. Of course, as John Paul II writes in *Veritatis Splendor*, such "obedience is not always easy. As a result of that mysterious original sin, committed at the prompting of Satan,... man's capacity to know the truth is also darkened, and his will to submit to it weakened. Thus, giving himself over to relativism and skepticism (*Jn* 18:38), he goes off in search of an illusory freedom apart from truth itself."

The dismal failure of this vain and often catastrophic search, is the essence of Chesterton's observation that Christianity can never be said to have failed because it has never been tried! We take his meaning. And yet... long ago before the Protestant heresy took root, when Catholic Europe knew that truth was knowable... perhaps, just once, it *was* tried. In an ancient time wracked with thoroughly modern dilemmas, on a glorious and grace-filled *Adventstag*, the ruling powers of a fledging Confederation - like a Jewish maid and a Swiss farmer's wife before them - said "yes" to God. "Yes!" to the right ordering of human beings to Christ through His Church as the sine qua non for social harmony.

From bitter personal experience of judicial, clerical and political corruption, bloody warfare and social upheaval within his own community, St. Nicholas knew well that this divine formula remains the pre-condition for lasting peace in every sphere of life. For obedience to that earthly authority - the Holy Catholic Church - is nothing less than obedience to the source of "all authority in Heaven and on earth", Jesus Christ, Who is God, and *"peace is always in God, for God is peace."* Amen!

BIBLIOGRAPHY

Christina Yates

Brother Klaus: Man of Two Worlds, The Ebor Press, York, 1989, pp.82.

R. Küchler-Ming

Saint Nicolas de Flüe, Benziger Verlag, Einsiedeln, 1981, pp.72.

Konstantin Volkinger

Bruder Klaus: Sein Leben, Bruder-Klausen-Stiftung, NZN Buchverlag, Zurich, 4th Ed., 1994, pp.212.

Father Cyril O.A.R.

Saint Nicholas of Flüe: Father of the Family, Politician, Mystic, St. Michael's Forest Valley Priory, Tajique, New Mexico, 1992, pp.24.

Inge M. Hugenschmidt-Thürkau

Ein Feuer das Brennt: Madame Curie und Dorothee von Flüe, Zwei Frauen - zwei Welten; Ein Stück fur eine Person, Verlag Aktuelle Texte, Heiligkreuztal, 1990, pp. 63.

Ida Lüthold-Minder

Von Himmel beglaubigt, (The sudden cure of Anna Melchior on the day of Brother Klaus' canonisation), Christiana Verlag, Stein am Rhein, 4th Editon, 1987, pp. 63.

SOME MAJOR HISTORICAL SOURCES

The Churchbook (*Kirchenbuch*) of Sachseln is the source of eyewitness statements by E. Rohrer, Heini am Grund, Oswald Isner, Hans von Flüe, Walter von Flüe and others. Most Churchbook translations quoted in this work are taken from Yates.

Dr. Robert Durrer   *BruderKlaus Die Ältesten Quellen über den seligen Niklaus von Flüe sein Leben und seinen Einfluss.* 2 vols. 1,300 pp. First published 1917 - 21. Obtainable in offset from Staatskanzlei Obwalden, 6060 Sarnen, Switzerland.

Walter Nigg   *Nicholas von Flüe Berichte der Zeitgenossen,* Patmos Verlag, Düsseldorf, 1962. Edited collection of the most important documents in Durrér (15th Cent German modernised).

Werner T. Huber   *Gespräch mit Bruder Klaus Der Pilgertrakt,* Edited and translated into modern German, Kanisius Verlag, Freiburg, 1987, pp. 51.

SELECTED LITERATURE

Werner T. Huber   *Dorothea Die Ehefrau des hl. Niklaus von Flüe,* Commentary on source material and texts from 1469-1993, Universitätsverlag, Freiburg, 1994, pp.320.

Roland Grobli	*Die Sehnsucht nach dem einig Wesen,* Life & teachings, NZN Verlag, Zurich, 1991, pp. 355.
Charles Journet	*Der heilige Niklaus von Flüe,*Classic theological work (also in French), Paulus Verlag, 1994, pp. 236.
Waltraud Herbstrith	*Bruder Klaus von Flüe : Meister des Gebets,* Visions & prayer life, Kafke Verlag, Frankfurt, 1978, pp. 80.
Fr. Phillipe Baud	*Nicolas de Flüe - 1417-1487 : Un silence qui fonde la Suisse,* Mixture of the spiritual and political history, Les editions du cerf, Paris, 1993, pp. 270.

AUDIOVISUAL

Gahwyler & Spichtig	*Saint Nicholas of Flüe :Open for God - Ready for Mankind,* Sachseln, 1993, 61 transparencies with cassette and text, 30 minutes, S.Fr. 120.

The Brother Klaus Fellowship was founded in 1927 by the Swiss bishops to encourage an interest in and devotion to Brother Klaus; to care for and preserve the places and buildings with which he is associated; to provide religious and general assistance to pilgrims, and to foster a wider knowledge of Brother Klaus through the provision of literature and other material. The work of the Fellowship is supported spiritually through the alliance in prayer of its members. Every Thursday, Holy Mass is celebrated for them at Brother Klaus' tomb in Sachseln. A Newsletter giving information of the current events is produced twice a year. There is an annual subscription of S.Fr 10 and one can join individually or as a family by writing to: Bruder-Klausen-Bund, Wallfahrts-Sekretariat, Dorfstrasse 11, Postfach 125, CH-6072, Sachseln OW.

BE PREPARED!

Read *Death of a Catholic Parish* and learn how a thriving Catholic parish:

- ᵛ Was divided against itself

- ᵛ Its Mass attedances halved

- ᵛ Its beautiful church defaced

- ᵛ Its liturgy debased

Death of a Catholic Parish
by
Michael McGrade

It issues a warning and prepares you to combat destructive elements in the Church today

£10 (incl. p&p - £12 Rep. Ireland) from PO Box 14754, London, SE19 2ZJ, England
(Cheques payable to *Christian Order*)
ISBN 0 646 06719 2